PASSING THE TORCH
SPORTSWOMEN WHO INSPIRE

THE MARY PETERS TRUST was established to create an ongoing and meaningful commemoration of Mary's Gold Medal win in the 1972 Olympic Games in Munich. The Trust supports talented young sportsmen and women, both able-bodied and disabled, from across Northern Ireland. It selects promising athletes, financially supports them and provides access to a team of experts who help and develop their pathway to success. For more than four decades the Mary Peters Trust has helped thousands of sportspeople to achieve their ambitions and enjoy the benefits of sport.

This book would not have been possible without the support of all those sportswomen who gave their stories. Lady Mary and the publishers would like to record their thanks to all who contributed, especially Her Royal Highness The Princess Royal, Patron of the Mary Peters Trust and a successful sportswoman in her own right. Thanks are also due to Derek Gallop for his help with the writing and editing, and to Gillian Hetherington at The Mary Peters Trust office in Belfast, and Cynthia Cherry, for their invaluable assistance in all matters, including contacting many of those involved.

LADY MARY PETERS

PASSING THE TORCH

SPORTSWOMEN WHO INSPIRE

GATEWAY PUBLISHING LIMITED

BUCKINGHAM PALACE

This is a book of short inspirational stories from a cross section of female athletes which will appeal to a wide audience. People can generally be divided into three groups: those who make things happen, those who watch things happen, and those who wonder what might have happened!

Those who know Mary Peters will immediately recognise that she belongs to the first group. Mary has attended 12 Olympic Games, including three as a competitor, two as a team manager, four with BBC NI Radio and one as a volunteer with the British Olympic Association, looking after sponsors, and as an Ambassador for the London Games.

Having won the gold medal at the Munich Olympics in 1972, at the age of 33, she raised the money to build a running track for her beloved Belfast and became a founder member of the Mary Peters Trust, assisting more than 4,000 young sports people to realise their dreams.

For 50 years she has been a voice and smiling face of athletics worldwide, fervently believing, whether you are a competitor, coach, commentator or campaigner, that sport matters, that sport inspires.

This book is designed to encourage more young women and girls to enjoy sport as a wonderful way to keep fit and healthy, make great friends and travel the world. I am sure you will enjoy reading it and that you will become inspired by the enthusiasm and real pleasure that radiate from Mary's personality in this book.

Anne

CONTENTS

Introduction 8

The Sportswomen

	SPORT	PAGE
Shirley Addison	ATHLETICS	10
Rebecca Adlington	SWIMMING	11
Clare Balding	HORSE RACING & PRESENTING	12
Sue Barker	TENNIS	14
Liz Barnes-Laban	ATHLETICS	16
Marzena Bogdanowicz	MULTISPORTS & ADMINISTRATION	18
Susan Boreham	ATHLETICS	20
Freya Bradshaw	ATHLETICS	21
Ann Brightwell	ATHLETICS	22
Lucy Bronze	FOOTBALL	24
Pam Brown	ATHLETICS & ADMINISTRATION	26
Lucy Bryan	ATHLETICS	27
Georgina Bullen	PARALYMPIC GOALBALL	28
Helen Burkart	ATHLETICS	31
Ita Butler	GOLF	32
Rosie Casals	TENNIS	34
Kathryn Christie	ATHLETICS	35
Nicole Cook	CYCLING	36
Maria Costello	MOTOCYCLE RACING	37
Pat Cropper	ATHLETICS	40
Sharron Davies	SWIMMING	42
Nisha Desai	ATHLETICS	44
Sophie Earley	TABLE TENNIS	46
Heide Ecker-Rosendahl	ATHLETICS	48
Tracy Edwards	SAILING	50
Verona Elder	ATHLETICS	51
Jessica Ennis-Hill	ATHLETICS	52
Non Evans	RUGBY UNION	54
Nicola Fairbrother	JUDO	55
Rachel Fenwick	ARCHERY	56
Donna Fraser	ATHLETICS	58
Mary Gordon-Watson	EVENTING	59
Katherine Grainger	ROWING	60
Janet Gray	WATER SKIING	62
Louise Greer	PARALYMPIC EQUESTRIANISM	66
Tanni Grey-Thompson	PARALYMPIC ATHLETICS	67
Sally Gunnell	ATHLETICS	70
Sylvia Harris	ARCHERY	72
Rachael Heyhoe Flint	CRICKET	73
Kate Hoey	POLITICS	74
Kelly Holmes	ATHLETICS	76
Wendy Houvenaghel	CYCLING	78
Cheriece Hylton	ATHLETICS	80
Shannon Hylton	ATHLETICS	82
Dorothy Hyman	ATHLETICS	85
Margaret Johnston	BOWLS	86
Shelley Jory-Leigh	POWERBOAT RACING	87
Shannon Kavanagh	TENNIS	92
Maeve Kyle	ATHLETICS & HOCKEY	95
Avril Lennox	GYMNASTICS	96
Gabby Logan	GYMNASTICS & PRESENTING	98
Rhona Martin	CURLING	99
Violet McBride	HOCKEY & GOLF	100
Shirley McCay	HOCKEY	101
Liz McColgan	ATHLETICS	102
Dianne McMillan	PARALYMPIC SWIMMING	103
Liz McVeigh	ROWING	104
Katharine Merry	ATHLETICS	106
Sheila Morrow	HOCKEY	108
Tina Muir	ATHLETICS	111
Hayley Murray	ATHLETICS	112
Aoife Ni Chaiside	CAMOGIE	113
Kerry O'Flaherty	ATHLETICS	116
Caroline O'Hanlon	NETBALL & GAELIC FOOTBALL	118
Sonia O'Sullivan	ATHLETICS	122
Christine Ohuruogu	ATHLETICS	124

Abi Oyepitan	ATHLETICS	126
Jo Pavey	ATHLETICS	128
Pauline Peel	ROWING	130
Mary Peters	ATHLETICS	131
Paula Radcliffe	ATHLETICS	140
Alison Ramsay	HOCKEY	142
Kate Richardson-Walsh	HOCKEY	144
Shirley Robertson	SAILING	146
Liz Rodgers	NETBALL	148
Susie Rodgers	PARALYMPIC SWIMMING	150
Freya Ross	ATHLETICS	152
Ann Sargent	ATHLETICS	153
Goldie Sayers	ATHLETICS	155
Diane Seaman	ATHLETICS	156
Wendy Sly	ATHLETICS	157
Janet Smith	ATHLETICS	158
Joyce Smith	ATHLETICS	159
Kelly Sotherton	ATHLETICS	160

Vicki Thomas	GOLF	161
Jayne Torvill	ICE DANCING	162
Christine Truman	TENNIS	164
Beth Tweddle	GYMNASTICS	165
Penelope Vincent-Sweet	ROWING	166
Fatima Whitbread	ATHLETICS	167
Steffi Wilson	ATHLETICS	169
Susie Wolff	MOTOR RACING	170
Isabel Woods	LONG-DISTANCE CYCLING	172
Pippa Woolven	ATHLETICS	174
Martine Wright	PARALYMPIC SITTING VOLLEYBALL	176
Francesca Zino	ROWING	178

Acknowledgement to Physicool	179
Acknowledgements & Imprint	180

INTRODUCTION

WHEN I went to the Olympic Games in Munich in 1972, I firmly believed that I could win the pentathlon gold medal. Not everyone was so confident.

I had already competed in two Olympics, finishing fourth in Tokyo in 1964 and a disappointing ninth in Mexico in 1968. Even though I struck gold at the 1970 Commonwealth Games in Edinburgh in both the shot and pentathlon – setting a Commonwealth record in the latter – few people in Great Britain & Northern Ireland had much expectation of my success two years later.

Significantly, as far as some observers were concerned, I would be 33 when the Games began and possibly 'past my best'.

When I applied for a scholarship from the Churchill Memorial Trust to help me go to California and train in heat for three months in the run-up to Munich, it was difficult to persuade my interviewers to share my vision of gold.

'Wasn't I bit long in the tooth to harbour ambitions like that?'

'Hadn't I been in athletics rather too long?'

'Didn't I think I was setting my sights just a little too high?'

No. It was precisely because of my age and having had so much experience that I felt I had a mature mind about success. I knew that all the hard work I had put in over so many years had been for a purpose.

Fortunately, the Trust approved my grant, and the warmth of my American experience contributed significantly to my ultimate success.

I simply set my mind on the top spot and on September 3, after an exhilarating competition and nail-biting finale, was crowned Olympic champion and World record-holder.

I would go on to win another cherished pentathlon gold medal for Northern Ireland in the Commonwealth Games in Christchurch, New Zealand in 1974 but, of course, the Olympic success was the pinnacle.

Those 36 hours of tense competition in Munich were the result of 20 years of preparation. It was my reward for the sort of commitment, dedication, determination and ambition that I hope to help instill in young sportswomen today through The Mary Peters Trust and this book.

My message to all young people is: If you have talent, or even if you haven't, have a go. The opportunities for friendship, travel and good health that sport gives is one which can never be replaced.

Painting a picture or singing a song doesn't give you the exposure to the world that sport does. I'd love every young person to have a go, even if they only enjoy it while they're at school and if you're a parent, be prepared to pass it on to your children too – the joy of taking part in sport.

Mary E. Peters

MARY PETERS

Munich Stadium 1972

SHIRLEY ADDISON

How I first became involved in sport

As the youngest of four children, sport was a way of life for my three older brothers and I. Rough and tumble began from birth. Before getting involved in athletics, my love was springboard and highboard diving, where I was British Masters Champion. Upon joining my local athletics club, North Shields Poly, I was quickly introduced to every event and enjoyed many a jam-packed weekend competing in as many events as I could to pick up points for the team. My medal cabinet had pride of place in the house! The buzz of getting PBs (personal bests) was my biggest driving force as an athlete.

Inspiration

Watching Denise Lewis win the Olympic Games heptathlon in 2000 was a huge inspiration. I'm amazed how people can master so many events, when I found it tough enough with only one to worry about.

I have a gorgeous photo and lovely memory of meeting Mary Peters as a spectator at an International Grand Prix at Gateshead Stadium when I was age 12.

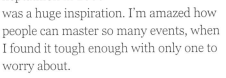

Memories

On one occasion, when diving was my main sport, my costume split in half – straight up the middle – when I hit the water. I was a self-conscious 13 year-old at the time and the costume 'malfunction' left nothing to the imagination!

I will always remember being landed with the name 'Battleaxe' as one of the Gladiators on the TV show. No matter how hard I tried to request a different name, 'Battleaxe' is what I became.

ACHIEVEMENTS

Commonwealth Games hammer (Manchester 2002)

Olympic Games (Athens 2004)

World Athletics Championships (Helsinki 2005)

Commonwealth Games (Melbourne 2006)

European Athletics Championships (Gothenburg 2006)

Scottish Record holder

Appeared as Battleaxe in TV show *Gladiators*

SWIMMING

REBECCA ADLINGTON OBE

How I first became involved in sport

I learned to swim when I was just three, so it was a natural progression for me to join a club when I was eight or nine. I loved swimming, and wanted to be in the water all the time. I saw it as a hobby rather than a 'job'. Because I started so young it was all I had ever known and all I wanted to do.

Inspiration

My family. As I come from a relatively small town (Mansfield) there was never a great role model that I looked up to. I have older sisters and simply wanted to be like them. I followed them everywhere. My parents were my greatest inspiration and support – they guided me in everything and helped me achieve my dream.

What I am doing now

I'm running my own learn-to-swim programme called Becky Adlington Swim Stars, and promoting the sport at any opportunity. I also work for the BBC as a TV pundit.

ACHIEVEMENTS

Olympic Games gold medals, 400m freestyle & 800m freestyle (Beijing 2008)

Olympic Games bronze medals, 400m freestyle & 800m freestyle (London 2012)

Commonwealth Games double gold medals, 400m freestyle & 800m freestyle (Delhi 2010)

Commonwealth Games double Bronze medals, 200m freestyle & 4 x 200m freestyle (Delhi 2010)

European Championships, one gold, one silver & one bronze (Budapest 2006 & 2010)

World Championships (long course) gold, 800m freestyle & silver, 400m freestyle (Shanghai 2011)

World Championships (short course) gold, 800m freestyle (Manchester 2008)

Appointed OBE in 2009

CLARE BALDING OBE
HORSE RACING & PRESENTING

How I first became involved in sport

I grew up in a racing yard (my father, Ian, was a racehorse trainer) so horses were all around us. I was definitely riding before I could walk. My dad was a passionate fan of all sports – cricket, rugby union, golf, football – so I was watching a lot all through my childhood.

Inspiration

There were not many female sports broadcasters on radio or TV when I started. Eleanor Oldroyd was hugely supportive and helpful, while Helen Rollason was also a major figure of inspiration, as she was the first woman to present Grandstand. Neither of them had come from a professional sporting background, which made me think it was possible to succeed as a broadcast journalist rather than an ex-pro.

Memories

My fondest memories will always be of London 2012. It was my fifth Olympic Games and fourth Paralympics so I was fairly well prepared for the intensity of the experience, and I had prepped extensively on both the history of the London Olympics and the variety of sports in 2012 compared to 1948 or 1908. I think it helped to have context and to understand the genesis of the Paralympic Games,

which effectively started at Stoke Mandeville in 1948 with the Wheelchair Games. I decided that I would immerse myself fully in the experience and to try to make viewers feel as if they were right there with me. I was so thrilled that everyone engaged so fully with the Games, and I look back on that summer with huge nostalgia. It felt like a simple, pure and hugely enjoyable summer where sport took over from grim headlines or tricky politics. It was magical.

When I was an amateur jockey years ago, I nearly knocked Princess Anne out of a race at Beverley. I didn't realize she was behind me on my inside when my horse jumped a path and cut across to the rail. It was a total mistake but it was over a mile from home. The stewards decided it wasn't worthy of an enquiry but, as I went on to win the race by a short head from HRH, she wasn't so sure and I fear she has never forgiven me.

In terms of broadcasting, live sport is always full of unexpected moments so you have to be quick on your feet. I have put my foot in it plenty of times but I always think that people understand you're not trying to mess things up, it's just that we all make mistakes. I'm much better now at apologising or laughing it off and moving on.

What I am doing now

I am a freelance broadcaster, working for a range of different TV stations on sport and factual documentaries. Since I stopped presenting horse racing I wanted to focus, where possible, on women's sport and have had a great time doing a women's football show for C4, Women's Super League matches for BT Sport, women's tennis for the BBC and BT, and I was involved in the closing ceremony of the 2019 Netball World Cup in Liverpool. It was a wonderful summer for women's sport and I really feel it has been a turning point in terms of respect and awareness. Now we need to make sure the investment follows and keep up the interest so that more girls can follow a career in sport.

I also write books for children and spend a lot of time travelling the country speaking at schools and Literary Festivals.

Clare interviewing the winners of the 2018 women's wheelchair tennis doubles at Wimbledon

ACHIEVEMENTS

It's not exactly *my* achievement and I am not claiming any credit for it, but I am most proud of being associated with aspects of sport that have a far wider impact than what happens on the field of play. Specifically, I believe very strongly that the improved coverage and increased investment in Paralympic sport and in women's sport will have far-reaching benefits.

Appointed OBE in 2013

BAFTA award for work on the 2012 London Olympics & Paralympics (2013)

Royal Television Society Sports Presenter of the Year (2003) & Presenter (2012)

Racing Journalist of the Year (2003) & Racing Broadcaster of the Year

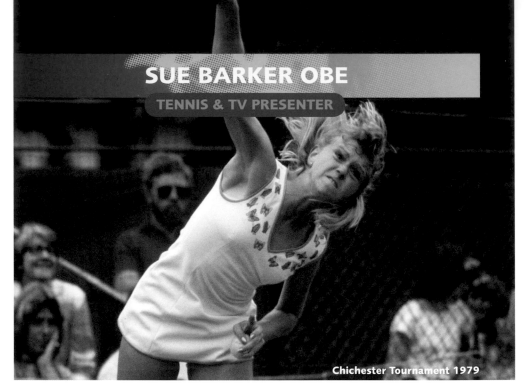

Chichester Tournament 1979

How I first became involved in sport

I came from a sports-mad family – we loved watching sport and playing it. When I was 12, I was spotted by a famous tennis figure in my area, Arthur Roberts, and he remained my coach throughout my career.

Inspiration

Mary Peters knows that she was my idol. I loved the way she competed. You could see that she had an iron will, a champion's mentality and looked like she always enjoyed the challenge. Billie Jean King was inspiring too. I not only admired her tennis but also how driven she was off the court and especially how, during the 1970s and against all the odds, she transformed women's tennis into a global sporting success story. That gave me the opportunity to play my 'hobby' as a career and I loved every minute of it.

CAREER RECORD:
Grand Slam Singles
Australian Open SF (1975, 1977)
French Open W (1976)
Wimbledon SF (1977)
World Ranking of No.3 (1977)
Grand Slam Doubles
Australian Open SF (1980, 1981)
Wimbledon SF (1978, 1981)
Grand Slam Mixed Doubles
French Open SF (1974)

Appointed OBE in 2015
Appointed MBE in 2000

Memories

I had always dreamed of playing on Centre Court at Wimbledon, the greatest tournament in the world. When I was competing there as a teenager, I was drawn against a legend and former champion, Maria Bueno, in the 2nd round. I was staying at the home of my good friend Linda Mottram in Wimbledon, and every morning we would scan the *Daily Telegraph*, which was the official newspaper for the tournament and the only way to find out the day's order of play.

I looked for my name but couldn't find it so decided to tuck in to a big breakfast before heading off to practise. As I was enjoying my food, Linda said: 'Are you nervous about playing on Centre Court?' My jaw dropped and I blurted out: 'What??'

I checked the paper again and there I was, second on after Bjorn Borg. Suddenly my appetite was gone and the nerves kicked in. On Centre Court and on television … 'Help!'

After Bjorn demolished his opponent, we were called. I was trembling as I walked out on to the world's most famous court. My knees were shaking so much I barely got up from the curtsey to the Royal Box.

However, after a very slow start, I began to enjoy the experience. I won the match in three sets and my love affair with Centre Court was under way.

In the 1990s, I used to host the BBC Wimbledon Highlights show with the former US tennis player, Pam Shriver. Every programme would finish with someone 'counting us down' to the end, by which time we had to have stopped talking. I was still getting used to this, trying to finish my words coherently by the time the count went to zero in my ear, but occasionally I would be rushed. One night I wanted to give a send-off to Steffi Graf who had announced her retirement, and the words I wanted to finish with were … 'so today we say a sad farewell to Steffi, but at least she leaves Wimbledon with some great memories.' Sadly, I was rushing a little that night, and said instead … 'so today we say a sad farewell to Steffi, but at least she leaves Wimbledon with some great mammaries.' Yes, it was very embarrassing and everyone laughed but, as many people pointed out, at least I was factually correct!

Sue interviewing for the BBC at Queen's Club 2018

LIZ BARNES-LABAN

How I first became involved in sport

I was very active as a child, so my mum fed me lots of bananas to replace the energy I spent chasing after my older brothers and sisters. They used to say 'Last one to that tree/caravan/lamp-post stinks' – I usually stank. My mum knew I was a fast runner, so she took me along to my local athletics club, Cambridge Harriers, where I was given the opportunity to excel. After that I left school and gave up.

At the age of 21, after living an unhealthy life involving alcohol, smoking and the rest, I decided that if I didn't try athletics again, I would never know how far I could have gone. I re-started from rock bottom in 1972.

Inspiration

If it wasn't for Cambridge Harriers Athletics Club, I doubt if I could have made it so far. Our first coach, Charlie Warner, laid the foundations for many club members to succeed in that era. Many went on to compete at national and international level.

Cliff Temple, the *Sunday Times* Athletics Correspondent, also played a major part in my return to athletics, and helped me through a difficult time after leaving school. After migrating to New Zealand I missed him, and intended to see him next time I visited the UK. However, he died before I got the chance and I've regretted it ever since.

Mary (Peters) always inspired me! I can remember watching the closing ceremony of the Munich Olympic Games, and thinking of how awesome it would be to be there.

I also trained with Frank Horwill's group at Crystal Palace for a while. One day, whilst we were doing our warm-up exercises, he belted out in his big Sergeant-Major voice: 'Liz Barnes! I want you to go home, take a piece of soap, and write in big letters on your mirror, '1976 or bust'!' I did and I didn't!

Memories

Despite spinal surgery, chronic fatigue, depression and many other minor ailments my torch still burns as brightly as ever. I was diagnosed with Ehlers Danlos Syndrome in my 60s and I was advised not to run. However, when I take my dog out for walks, I can't help but break into a jog from time to time. I can't resist running down the beach towards the sea, jogging round a grassy field, or trotting on a carpet of pine needles in the forest. My heart nearly bursts out of its chest, and my joints seize up afterwards,

ACHIEVEMENTS

English Schools 800m Champion & record-holder (1969)

South African 800m Champion & record-holder (1975)

Olympic Games GB representative 800m & 4 x 400m relay (Montreal 1976)

UK 800m Champion (1978)

Commonwealth Games, 4th 800m (Edmonton 1978)

European Championships, semi-finalist, 800m (Prague 1978)

UK Indoor 400m champion (1979) 800m champion (1980)

European Indoor Championships bronze medal, 800m (Sindelfingen 1980)

Ran the London Marathon aged 60 (It took me five hours!)

but it's worth it, just to feel the wind in my face, a stretch in my stride, and the feeling that I could run forever.

I recall getting to the start of an Inter-Club 400m race, and was about to strip off my track pants when I realized I'd forgotten to put my shorts on.

Being quite short-sighted, I was always put on the first leg of the relay – just in case I couldn't spot the person I was taking the baton from or handing it to! Eventually I swallowed my pride and wore glasses.

I still have dreams about forgetting my shorts, missing the bus back to the airport because I'm frantically still packing my bags, losing my way back to the hotel, and dreaming I'm in the Olympics – all at the same age I am now. However, there is no way I could ever run twice round the track in two minutes!

MARZENA BOGDANOWICZ

How I first became involved in sport

Two of my brothers were always sporty, they introduced me to volleyball and football. My father could not understand my enthusiasm for sport, but let me get on with it. So I did!

Sport makes you feel alive. It builds lasting friendships and trust, and keeps you young and healthy. It makes global friendships and crosses international barriers, is multinational and in a language that transcends ethnicity, religion and age.

Inspiration

Daley Thompson. I recall watching him at the Olympic Games and thought he was amazing, as were Nadia Comaneci and Olga Korbut in gymnastics.

Memories

I have a particularly vivid one of Mary Peters, with a Union Jack on her head, waving flags and running around the outside of the boxing ring after Audley Harrison won his gold medal in Sydney in 2000!

What I am doing now

I am still working in sport, as I have done continuously since I was a student, and am still passionate about it and the part it plays in all our lives.

I joined The FA in 2017 as Head of Marketing and Commercial, Women's Football. I have worked on an amazing Lionesses' 2019 World Cup campaign, a successful English bid for the 2021 UEFA Women's EURO, and secured multi-million pound support for women's football from Barclays.

Prior to that I ran my own consultancy in sports marketing, sponsorship and event management and between 1996 and 2006 I was the inaugural Director of Marketing at the British Olympic Association. As well as building the BOA's first commercial and marketing department I was the architect of the Team GB brand, a legacy I am proud to have left behind.

ACHIEVEMENTS

Mine are small scale compared to Mary Peters ... no gold medals, Olympic or World records. However, sport has led me to my current position at The Football Association (FA).

I have completed two Ironman events (not sure why I agreed to the second!) and many triathlons. Also, two London Marathons, numerous half-marathons, 10km and 5km races and many cycling events. One of my toughest sporting achievements was the Trans-Portugal Mountain Bike Race – 1000km over eight days riding from North to South Portugal on a 90per cent off-road terrain of mountains, trails, hills, streams and sand.

ATHLETICS
CROSS-COUNTRY & DISTANCE

SUSAN BOREHAM

How I first became involved

Sport has always played a very significant part in my life. At Victoria College, my school in Belfast, I was inspired by my PE teacher Ann Morrison to participate in as many activities as possible. These included hockey, badminton, squash, athletics and tennis. I suppose you could say I was a Jill-of-all-trades and master of none. Every afternoon I was involved in extra-curricular activities. At Queen's University, Belfast I continued to play both hockey and squash and represented the university in the UK and Ireland. The least said about those trips the better!

Inspiration

At QUB I met my future husband Colin, a GB and Northern Ireland decathlete. Sport brought us together as we trained in the same area. Quickly I realized that if you want to spend time with an athlete, you need to get involved in athletics. Not being the fastest thing on two feet, I worked out that I had to choose an event where I could just outrun the opposition. That was what I did in 1982 to win the ladies section of the first Belfast Marathon, having only taken up the sport two years previously. It was a fantastic experience. Belfast had a pretty poor reputation worldwide and it felt good to take part in the marathon trend which was sweeping the rest of the world. As

ACHIEVEMENTS

Belfast Marathon, winner (women) 1982
Cross-country, represented Northern Ireland, home international

the Belfast marathon was over two laps there was plenty of support encouraging everyone all the way round. Colin's idea of encouragement was to ask me why it had taken so long to complete the first lap!

Memories

Sport has continued to influence my life ever since. I am a PE teacher at Fort Hill College, Lisburn; my husband is a Professor of Sports Science; our children all keep fit and Adam has represented Ireland at the U23 World Rowing Championships. Now I keep fit with the occasional jog and try to hit a ball round a golf course.

Although given the chance I would have loved to have gone to an Olympic Games or major competition, I have thoroughly enjoyed everything sport has given to me. It has brought richness to my life and friends that will stay with me forever.

ATHLETICS

FREYA BRADSHAW

How I first became involved in sport

My teacher just put me down for the cross-country team at school. From there I joined my local athletics group and I became a bit obsessed with it all!

Inspiration

Kelly Holmes was my great inspiration. She won her double Olympic gold medals in Athens just as I began training and I just thought, 'Wow, I want to do that!' My dad drove me and my sister to Sheffield one day after school, to one of her public appearances, and it made me want to achieve something similar to what she did in the Olympics even more. I was given one of her books, *My Olympic 10 days* and whenever I didn't feel in the mood for training, I'd read a couple of pages and it would turn my mood around instantly. It made me eager to get on the track and run hard.

Memories

I remember falling over a lot of hurdles and out of blocks over the years! Also getting really shy when I bumped into athlete Eilidh Child at the British Championships. She asked me which heat I was in and I just went bright red, mumbled something and walked away really quickly. I wish I'd acted a bit cooler!

ACHIEVEMENTS
England U20 400m hurdles finalist (2014)
English Schools Championships, 4th 400m hurdles (2012)
British Colleges 400m & 400m hurdles champion (2012)

ANN BRIGHTWELL MBE (NÉE PACKER)

How I first became involved in sport

At primary school I found I could beat the other children at games of 'tag' and outrun them in casual, friendly races. Sport was a valued part of the curriculum at my co-educational grammar school, and encouraged by both male and female staff. I couldn't get enough of it, whether it was hockey, netball, tennis or athletics. Sport was both enjoyable and challenging, and offered me an opportunity to excel.

Inspiration

The grammar school staff inspired me to pursue my talent at a time when female participation in sport was not as fashionable as it is today. I was vaguely aware of the 1948 Olympics in London and the achievements of Fanny Blankers-Koen (Dutch sprinter) which lingered in my psyche. After I won the 100m at the English Schools Championships in 1959, I was certainly inspired by the Easter course at Lilleshall for outstanding young athletes. It was where I met Dennis Watts, who would coach and advise me thereafter. But my biggest inspiration was my then fiancé (now husband) Robbie Brightwell, who showed me that natural talent was not enough and that only hard work and specific training would produce world-class performances.

Memories

Whilst training to be a teacher at Dartford PE College, some of the girls managed to obtain early samples of fake tan. Confident that it would enhance my appearance on the track, I applied some prior to an international meeting at the White City. Sadly, the application proved 'hit & miss'. The liquid, which was transparent and put on with a 'wand', was supposed to develop overnight. On the morning of the meeting, I resembled a brown-and-white zebra and kept my tracksuit on until the last possible moment before my race. Not even filling in the white lines with makeup could improve my appearance so, full of embarrassment, I stripped off and then just ran my fastest!

**Ann Packer winning the 800 Metres Gold
Medal in the 1964 Tokyo Olympics**

ACHIEVEMENTS

**Olympic Games gold medal, 800m
(Tokyo 1964)**

**Olympic Games silver medal, 400m
(Tokyo 1964)**

Appointed MBE in 1965

**Inducted into the England Athletics
Hall of Fame, 2009**

LUCY BRONZE

How I first became involved in sport

My family has always been very active and my parents wanted me to do as many sports as possible. My mum always sided with me in my choice to play tennis, but I realized whilst quite young I wasn't suited to individual sports, whereas I had played football with my older brother since I was four and I loved everything he loved!

Inspiration

I never really had sporting heroes growing up as I didn't watch a lot of TV. My family has always been the biggest influence on my sports career, my mum in particular always inspired me to push myself. She is one of the few people who has always believed in me, and probably why I feel inspired by her.

In terms of sporting personalities, as I learned more about women's football, Kelly Smith was always a name mentioned, and for all the right reasons. At points in her career she was the best in the world at what she does. I now want to be the best, I'll never reach the highs of Kelly but it is inspiring to know someone who has pushed those boundaries.

Memories

One of my best sporting memories would have to be from when I was still a kid, and a story my mum and auntie especially love. I must have been 10 or 11, playing on a boys' team against boys' teams, and my auntie, who is quite a feminist, took me to Wallsend in Newcastle for one of my games. The other team – well, one boy in particular – found it funny that my team had a girl playing for them. I was pretty shy as a child, so didn't say anything, just waited for the game to kick off. Basically by the end of the game this same boy was 'crying like a little girl' because all game I had run rings round him and kept him off the ball. Not the funniest story, but certainly one of the most satisfying!

What I am doing now

I played for Manchester City from 2014 until 2017, a club which has some of the best facilities in the world. Since last year I have been playing for Olympique Lyonnais in France. 🌱

ACHIEVEMENTS

England international player since 2013, making more than 70 appearances

Women's World Cup, represented England (2015, 2019)

Playing for my country in the sport I love is my biggest achievement, one that not many people have the opportunity to do. Within that, playing for England at a World Cup in 2015, where we finished 3rd through a rollercoaster of games is something I know I won't forget in a hurry. I exceeded all expectations, scoring big goals in big games.

ATHLETICS & ADMINISTRATION

PAM BROWN

How I first became involved in sport

I loved sport at school but what was on offer was very limited ... rounders and tennis in the summer, hockey and netball in the winter. During my last year at school, I met a man who was involved in coaching athletics and got talked into trying it. Believe me, it was hard work. I didn't realize that playing school netball gave you no fitness so I was on my knees for months. However, I persevered and after the man and I moved from Lancashire to Northern Ireland and I had our son, I started training in earnest.

Inspiration

I had three: Sean Kyle & Maeve Kyle and Mary Peters. Sean was my coach for a good while and if he told me I could do something, I believed him! He was truly inspirational. Maeve looked after me at the beginning of my career and gave me many important tips, such as how to run downhill and how to spit when running without wrapping it round myself! I loved the way Mary handled her fame, and I still do.

Memories

I remember lining up for an 800m at Stretford track in Manchester, possibly a Northern Counties event. I had travelled over from Northern Ireland with my husband and young son (probably about three at the time) and they were standing just beyond the start/finish line watching me. I was very nervous, as was everyone else, and tensions were high. The starter said, 'On your marks' and we trotted to the line ready for the gun. There was a loud bang and we all started sprinting for the first bend. Suddenly, there was another gunshot – a recall. We all stopped and walked back, looking at each other in bewilderment. Who had false started? That never happened in an 800m race. We got back to the start and the starter looked as bewildered as we did. He shook his head, apologised and set us off again. After the race had finished there was much discussion about what had happened, but none of the officials seemed to know. It was only when I got to my son and saw him holding a string with a bit of red rubber at the end of it and my husband trying to stop laughing that I realized what had happened. What a time for a balloon to pop! 🔥

ACHIEVEMENTS

Northern Ireland Champion, 400m, 800m, 1500m, 3,000m & cross-country (1970s)

Commonwealth Games competitor (Edmonton 1978)

Athletics UK Official

Athletics Technical Official at the following Commonwealth Games:

Victoria, Canada 1994; Kuala Lumpur 1998; Manchester 2002 & Glasgow 2014

Olympic Games, London 2012

ATHLETICS
POLE VAULT

LUCY BRYAN

How I first became involved in sport

I come from a family where sport was encouraged from a young age, and it played an important part in family life. I started with gymnastics and swimming at primary school but had the opportunity at senior school to try indoor athletics. I stopped gymnastics because I joined the local athletics club (Bristol & West AC). It was my PE Teacher, Karen Price, who had encouraged me to try athletics. I tried various events but once I had given the pole vault a go I knew I wasn't going to try any more events because I enjoyed it so much!

ACHIEVEMENTS

World Youth Championships, bronze medal (Lille 2011)

European U23 bronze medal (Bydgoszcz 2017)

Many National titles at U15, U17 & U20 level

British Championship, silver medal

GB Commonwealth Games team (Gold Coast 2018)

Inspiration

Karen was my initial inspiration for starting athletics. She encouraged me right from the start all the way through school and even now, although I am no longer at school, she still keeps in touch. I have many athletes that I look up to including Fabiana Murer and Renaud Lavillenie. However, my main inspiration has to come from my family, especially my brother Joe who is a professional footballer (formerly Bristol City, now with Fulham FC). Seeing his dedication and drive has spurred me on to always try to be better.

GEORGINA BULLEN

PARALYMPIC GOALBALL

How I first became involved in sport

I always attended mainstream school, despite being registered as blind, but I never really thought I was very good at sport. No one wants the girl on their team who can't see the ball, yet still goes sprinting towards the crowd with her hockey stick flying around. In fact, I was actively discouraged from it by my teachers as they told me I wouldn't be able to handle GCSE PE.

When I was 14, I was invited along to a Paralympic talent identification day and I just thought I'd give it a go. To my surprise, from that day, I was fast-tracked straight onto the GB Women's Goalball team (a sport I'd never heard of previously) and was instantly training with and against the best men and women in the country.

Although I was shockingly awful at it to begin with, I just got the bug. Unlike other disability sports I had tried, Goalball was quick and brutal and it got my adrenaline pumping. Every time I played, I found it completely addictive. It developed in me a sense of competitiveness that I hadn't been aware of before and I just loved the feeling of winning. Also, I absolutely loved being part of a team.

Inspiration

It was my team mates who inspired me because they just made everything look so easy! I wasn't used to having my sight taken away, so at first, I really struggled to remain relaxed. However, they all seemed so composed and awesome, I just wanted to be like them and be then able to give other people the supportive and encouraging impact my team mates had on me.

Memories

No one really knows what Goalball is, so we're used to a maximum crowd of maybe 200. However, when we entered the Copper Box at the 2012 Olympics we had 7,000 people there cheering for us as host nation – it was literally like being swallowed up by a wall of noise. When we came out to play China, I was nervous enough already, but seeing the crowds made me super nervous. I remember saying to myself, 'Don't let the first shot in' and 'don't have a little bladder accident in front of 7,000 people!'

What I am doing now

I am still a starting line-up player for the GB Women's Goalball team, but I also run my own business, called Team Insight. We deliver corporate team building and visual impairment awareness training events, using Goalball and other blindfolded activities.

ACHIEVEMENTS

Member GB Women's Goalball
team since 2009 (at age 14)

Paralympic Games,
Quarter-finalist (London 2012)

European Championships,
team gold (2009)

The mood was great, people were buoyant, the excitement was palpable, and anything that stood still was painted orange and white. The pride in the team, and how that filtered down to the people in the streets, was amazing.

Caroline O'Hanlon

I was competing in a world full of men and it was tough. No one wanted to be beaten by a woman, least of all teammates, and they made that clear. That was inspiration in itself for me to do a fantastic job.

Susie Wolff

I once had a marriage proposal at mile 17 of the Chicago Marathon. I didn't accept!

Paula Radcliffe

ATHLETICS

HELEN BURKART

Inspiration

I am always inspired by people who are nice, caring beings – those who work hard and through it achieve their goals, or do their best to achieve them. This is regardless of their field of work. I always admired sports people whom I respected, either through meeting them, on and off their field of activity, or through their character in interviews. They always helped others, just by being who they were.

Memories

We were at an International GB meeting and Sharon Gibson, Tessa Sanderson, Vanessa Head and myself were to share a room. Sharon, Vanessa and I went upstairs, while Tessa was downstairs. We got the best beds and left Tessa with what we call the 'hospital bed' (that sort of extra bed that is sometimes shoved in a shared room). Of course, Tessa wasn't happy when she came upstairs. She tried to pull Sharon off the bed she was sitting on. Of course, NONE of us budged/moved and we won out in the end. We were all laughing.

I hope it brings back happy memories to these three people … if they remember it! 🎽

ACHIEVEMENTS

Olympic Games semi-finalist 4 x 100m
(Los Angeles 1984)

Commonwealth Games 200m
(Brisbane 1982)

Commonwealth Games 400m
(Edinburgh 1986)

European Championships semi-finalist 400m
(Stuttgart 1986)

"We got the best beds and left Tessa with what we call the 'hospital bed" …"

GOLF

ITA BUTLER (NÉE BURKE)

How I first became involved in sport

When my parents came to live in Dublin in the late 1950s we joined Elm Park Golf Club in Donnybrook. The members of Elm Park, both men and women, could not have been more supportive and the men there even invited me to play in some of their competitions at the weekends. This was unheard of as women could not become full members of golf clubs in Ireland. At that time women could only be associate members and as a result they did not have access to most golf courses at weekends. I was so fortunate to have had such a progressive and supportive club.

My first introduction to a structured coaching scheme came in 1960 when I was identified, together with five other girls, as having 'potential'. This group was made up of four girls from Northern Ireland and two girls from Southern Ireland and we were part of an ILGU/LGU drive to improve the standard of women's golf in Great Britain and Ireland.

The fact that this coaching scheme was arranged around weekends was in itself a novel idea, certainly in Ireland, and that it was to take place at one of Ireland's most outstanding golf clubs, Royal Portrush Golf Club in Co. Antrim, made it particularly special.

ACHIEVEMENTS

Individual

Leinster Champion (1962, 1963, 1964 & 1967)

Midland Champion (1964)

Munster Champion (1965)

Irish Ladies Close Championship, runner up (1972 & 1978)

US Amateur Open Championship qualified (32 to qualify – lost to winner Joanne Gunderson Carner, Pittsburg, USA (1966)

President & Chairman Irish Ladies' Golf Union 2003 & 2004

Inspiration

It was at Portrush that I first came into contact with P.G. 'Stevie' Stevenson who was the professional there at the time. Apart from being introduced to female golfers of my own age, one of the things I liked most was the fact that Stevie coached each one of us on an individual basis. All six of us had very different styles of play and Stevie did not deem it necessary or wise to undertake a 'one method fits all' approach to teaching. Instead he focused on each of our strengths and then found ways to eliminate our weaknesses.

Stevie managed to make coaching such an enjoyable experience. Even though I later had coaching from World-renowned professionals I always found myself returning to Stevie's advice. As a direct result of this particular coaching scheme, I was inspired to compete in events that led to being selected to play for Ireland and GB & I teams. Indeed, it opened up a whole new world to me.

What I am doing now

The benefits of sport, when played in the right spirit, are evident to most people – in terms of health, lifestyle, exercise, friendship and learning how to cope with success and failure. This has been brought home to me again through my involvement as a volunteer with the Special Olympic Golf Coaching Group at my golf club, Elm Park. This particular group is one of the most competitive group of athletes I have had the privilege of being involved with. Indeed, I was so impressed with their fierce, competitive spirit, which they combined with a wonderful and generous sporting attitude towards their fellow competitors that, in 2007 I donated a trophy to be played for annually. This trophy is awarded to the player who, in the opinion of the Committee, has shown greatest endeavour and sporting attitude over the previous season.

ROSIE CASALS

How I first became involved in sport

I had a lot of energy as a child and happened to be introduced to tennis by my father who played recreational tennis at Golden Gate Park in San Francisco. I was about 8 or 9 and I loved it; I don't remember when I couldn't hit a tennis ball. It was a great feeling and I loved to play in tennis tournaments. Eventually I was ranked at the top in juniors and No.1 in my age group in Northern California.

Inspiration

The first time I travelled out of the country was in 1966. I played doubles with Billie Jean King, was introduced to Wimbledon and Centre Court and fell in love with it. We didn't win that year, but we did in 1967. The game of tennis has been my inspiration and it has been a great sport and life for me. It made me who I am today, and I am grateful.

Memories

Once when were playing as professionals in the George McCall Tennis League, we were in France and had taken our gear to the local launderette. Unfortunately, it closed before we got back – and we were leaving first thing in the morning for another town. It took us hours to locate the owner and convince him to open up the launderette again and let us get our clothes. He wasn't happy – but we could hardly have left without our tennis garbs and underwear!

What I am doing now

I own my own sports company, Sportswoman Inc. I organise exhibitions, corporate clinics and charity tennis events. I work with many of my contemporaries and some of the men legends. I also established a Tennis Foundation in the Coachella Valley (Palm Springs area of California) to support Junior Tennis. I am busy helping juniors by coaching them and raising money.

ACHIEVEMENTS

Grand Slam Singles
Australian Open SF (1967)
French Open QF (1969, 1970)
Wimbledon SF
(1967, 1969, 1970, 1972)
US Open F (1970, 1971)

Grand Slam Doubles
Australian Open F (1969)
French Open F (1968, 1970, 1982)
Wimbledon W
(1967, 1968, 1970, 1971, 1973)
US Open F
(1967, 1971, 1974, 1982)

Grand Slam Mixed Doubles
Australian Open SF (1969)
French Open SF (1969, 1970, 1972)
Wimbledon W (1970, 1972)
US Open W (1975)

Team competitions
Federation Cup W (1970, 1976, 1977, 1978, 1979, 1980, 1981)
Wightman Cup W (1967, 1976, 1977, 1979, 1980, 1981, 1982)

ATHLETICS

KATHRYN CHRISTIE

How I first became involved in sport

I love being active. I enjoy training and get a kick out of seeing hard work pay off. To me, sport is the best way to stay fit, healthy and focused and I find it teaches me life lessons on how to plan and manage my time. At university I had to be very productive with my time. I enjoyed going to training as it allowed me to put my focus towards training and getting a break from studying.

Inspiration

My cousin, international swimmer Kerry Buchan, has been through lots in her life such as injuries and the loss of a close family member. She did her best to qualify for the Commonwealth Games in Glasgow 2014 (which would have been her third Games) but unfortunately, she was just fractions off the qualifying time. To me she is inspirational.

Memories

When I was under 15, I was warming up for the Scottish Championships 200m semi-final, and I decided to put my leg up on a hurdle as part of a warm-up stretch as I'd seen older athletes doing it before. I ran in the semi and won it to qualify for the final, however my leg didn't feel quite right and I couldn't do the final.

Later on my dad asked me if I had done anything that 'may have caused the strain' and I said not. However, it soon clicked that the 'leg-on-the-hurdle' moment caused the hamstring strain, simply because I had never done it before and the hurdle was rather high! My dad remembers me saying: 'but all the professionals do it'. It taught me at a young age to stick to what I know!

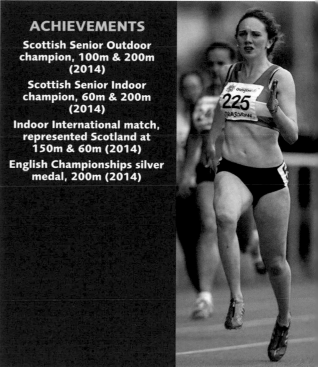

ACHIEVEMENTS

Scottish Senior Outdoor champion, 100m & 200m (2014)

Scottish Senior Indoor champion, 60m & 200m (2014)

Indoor International match, represented Scotland at 150m & 60m (2014)

English Championships silver medal, 200m (2014)

CYCLING

NICOLE COOKE MBE

How I first became involved in sport

I became involved in cycling when I was young, for all the freedom and adventure that is possible riding a bike. I loved exploring the lanes where I lived and discovering the great outdoors. I have a competitive nature, and was always interested in cycling races. After initially asking my parents to take me to some races, I simply loved it.

Memories

What I really love about sport is the endless opportunities it gives you, if you are prepared to work hard. The more you put in the more you can get out and this has always spurred me on to give my very best.

ACHIEVEMENTS

Olympic Games gold medal (Beijing 2008)

World Championships gold medal (Varese 2008)

Commonwealth Games gold medal (Manchester 2002)

Tour de France, winner (2006 & 2007)

Giro D'Italia, winner (2004)

World Cup Series, winner (2003 & 2006)

Appointed MBE in 2009

Nicole Cooke being interviewed by TV presenter Angharad Mair, Cardiff Bay

MARIA COSTELLO MBE

How I first became involved in sport

I grew up in a small village outside Northampton, so when I left school I needed transport to get to and from my first job as a veterinary nurse. I bought a second-hand Honda Melody scooter with a little top-box on the back that had absolutely no street credibility. My parents wanted me to buy a car but I got myself a Yamaha TZR125. I used to race around the country lanes with a group of lads that met in my village. We all rode to Mallory Park to spectate at my first race meeting. I fell in love with the sport. I was thrown off my road bike and into a brick wall when a pensioner with poor eyesight pulled their car out of a side road directly in front of me, causing me to have a broken pelvis, elbow, knee and ribs. The upside was the compensation I received from the crash which funded my first race bike, a Suzuki RGV250. My first race was a club meeting at Mallory Park in 1995.

Inspiration

My parents were vehemently opposed to me racing, but I'd always been an independent person. When I started racing, my parents were so against me racing that I banned them from watching me. Their lack of support fuelled my desire to succeed. Then they arrived unannounced at a race and gradually they started to understand that this was more than a faze and came around to having a daughter who raced motorcycles. I've had many people inspire and support me over the years, people like Dave Weston, who was my mentor at the start. Joining Sandra Barnett's (former fastest woman at the TT) all-female team was instrumental in igniting my love of the TT when the team took me to compete in the Isle of Man Manx Grand Prix. It was Sandra who stood out at the very first race I went to watch and who showed me that women can compete. Also never forgetting the incredible giant of a racer and TT legend, Dave Jefferies, who gave me some grounding advice to always go out and enjoy riding my race bike, especially at the TT. He made me increase my practice laps and he always came to my van because he knew I would have cake, and he once lent me his old Mercedes van to enable me to do a TT one year. His advice still runs through my head before I set off down Bray Hill to this day.

Memories

I've had many highs and lows (including 24 broken bones), but becoming the ⇒

ACHIEVEMENTS

5 Isle of Man Classic TT Silver replicas (2014–2017)

1 Isle of Man Classic TT Bronze Replica (2015)

8 Isle of Man TT Bronze replicas (2004–2017)

5 Isle of Man Manx Grand Prix Silver replicas (2002–2017)

Fastest woman ever at the Manx Grand Prix (2002)

Fastest woman ever at the Isle of Man TT, lapping the TT course at 114.73mph – Guinness World record (2004)

First solo female to get a podium finish in a race around the Isle of Man TT course, at the Manx Grand Prix (2005)

Fastest woman to lap the North West 200 (2016)

Fastest woman to lap at the Ulster Grand Prix (2016)

3rd place podium finish in the Classic 500cc TT race – the highest placed solo female in the history of the Classic TT (2016)

Appointed MBE in 2009

first woman to stand on the podium in a race around the Isle of Man TT course was something special. I finished third in the 2005 Ultra-Lightweight race on a Tim Bradley RLR RVF400 at the Manx Grand Prix.

In 2009, I became the first (and, so far, only) female motorcycle (solo) racer to receive an MBE. On a day of drama, I left my Northampton home in a car with my parents and sister but arrived at Buckingham Palace without them, as bad traffic forced me to leave them on the side of the road in my car, as I was taken on the back of a motorbike. When I was presented to the Prince of Wales, he asked me whether I had arrived on a motorbike and I laughed and said 'Yes, I did arrive on a motorbike!' Happily, my family had made it in time. I was so thankful of this as having them there meant everything to me. My dad had taken over the driving and the police had basically let them park on the lawn of Buckingham Palace to get them in on time.

Holding the fastest female lap record at all three international road races is something I'm hugely proud of, but even more so is my podium finish at the 2016 Isle of Man Senior Classic TT on the Beugger Racing Paton, made even more momentous because I stood next to my hero, and 23 times TT winner and the winner of the race, John McGuinness. Even as I was reading pit boards telling me that I was third on the road I said out loud in my own helmet, 'I hope John is winning', as sharing the podium with him was an incredible career highlight.

Racing has opened many doors for me and among the many unexpected experiences I've had is becoming an animated character in a PlayStation game, a rider double for Reese Witherspoon in a Hollywood movie and also becoming a published author.

What I am doing now

I'm becoming a regular guest speaker/ presenter for a number of organisations and functions, and this is something I enjoy and on which I have had very positive feedback. It's great that my story can cross over to so many fields and help motivate, stimulate and entertain everyone from school children to business CEOs. If you'd had told me when I was a girl that I would be hosting Gala dinners and motorcycle launches, talking at Scotland Yard and in front of audiences of up to a thousand people, I never would have believed it!

I'm still competing on modern motorcycles and sidecars. I also compete on classic motorcycles for BMW Group Classic, and at the Classic TT onboard a privately owned Paton 500 for Beugger Racing.

I am actively involved in supporting women who wish to ride and race, and I founded the group Woman on a Motorcycle to encourage and promote confidence among female riders. I have pioneered 'women only' trackdays since 2013, and this is something I would love to take around the world. Being a motorcycle racing ambassador for Susie Wolff's 'Dare to Be Different' campaign enables me to educate young women about the sport. I've worked as a mentor for the young riders competing in the European Junior Cup and been a member of the FIM Women in Motorcycling commission.

I am an IAM RoadSmart road safety ambassador and in November 2018 I became the first woman in the 67-year history of the TT Riders Association to be appointed president. I will promote this worthy organisation as much as possible over the next year.

ATHLETICS

PAT CROPPER MBE (NÉE LOWE)

How I first became involved in sport

I found I was very competitive at a young age. This came from both of my parents – my father was a footballer, my mother the youngest of six children! I had a PE teacher, when I entered grammar school, who was not a great instructor but somehow encouraged me into all school sport. Once in the 6th form I had a very enthusiastic and progressive PE teacher who gave lots of time to my training. I went to the All-England Schools Championships where I was 3rd in the 150yds. I also played county, regional and England U21 hockey and county tennis

Inspiration

I was at Chelsea College of PE when Anne Packer (Brightwell) won her gold medal in Tokyo (1964). I was truly inspired with her run especially as I had been very fortunate to meet her and indeed share a room with her prior to this. She was and still is a lovely person, and a great ambassador for sport.

Memories

This is difficult because what is really amusing at the time is often not so when retold and out of context. However, when I had been selected to compete against the USSR in the late 1960s the famous

40

Pat with the victorious 4 x 400m relay team at the 1969 European Athletics Championships in Athens. (L to R) Lillian Board, Rosemary Stirling, Pat Lowe and Janet Simpson

Press sisters were on the USSR team. I was queuing for the toilet at the old White City Stadium, along with several other athletes – both Brits and Russians – when there was an almighty grunt and clatter. We all turned to look at each other wondering whatever had happened and out came Tamara Press, a very large, muscular athlete, to say the least, with the toilet chain in her hand. She promptly dropped it onto the floor and in a very deep voice uttered words in Russian and grunted her way out of the room. It could have been somewhat scary, but we could see the funny side of this enormous woman wrecking the lavatory, and we all broke down in laughter at what we had experienced.

ACHIEVEMENTS

Olympic Games finalist, placed 6th, 800m (Mexico 1968)

European Championships gold medal & world record, 4 x 400m (Athens 1969)

European Championships silver medal, 800m (Helsinki 1971)

Commonwealth Games silver medal, 800m (Edinburgh 1970)

Member of five world record-breaking relay teams, including 3 x 880yds, 3 x 800m, 4 x 800m, 4 x 400m

Appointed MBE in 1974

SWIMMING

SHARRON DAVIES MBE

How I first became involved in sport

As a child I was always sporty. By the time I was eight I had given up all my other activities to concentrate on swimming, training most days in the pool, even though I had broken both wrists in a childhood accident. I swam for GB for the first time at the age of 11, and at the Olympics aged 13.

Inspiration

Mark Spitz. I remember watching him on TV in 1972 winning his seven Olympic gold medals, and thinking, 'Wow, I'd like to do that'. I also had the privilege of swimming with Australian Shane Gould and ex-Tarzan and Olympian Johnny Weissmuller, when I was first starting out. I admired many British sporting stars, including Mary Peters, and I remember David Wilkie (Olympic champion, 1976) coming to a pool when I was young and showing me his medals.

> " I was the youngest one on the 1976 GB Olympic team at 13, ... "

Memories

I have a special memory of sharing a flat in Seoul at the 1988 Olympic Games.

I was thinking of coming back into swimming after an almost forced eight-year break from competition and training, due to trust fund and amateur rules. Mary Peters, who was my roommate as we were both working for NZ radio, sat me down and encouraged me, saying I wouldn't want to go through life thinking, 'what if'. So, I got back in the pool at the ripe old age of 28 and did four more years. I was the youngest one on the 1976 GB Olympic team at 13, and the oldest in Barcelona at almost 30. By then I had broken more British records and picked up two more Commonwealth Games medals.

What I am doing now

I am now involved in TV, motivational and hosting work as well as being a qualified personal trainer, particularly interested in children's health and fitness issues.

ACHIEVEMENTS	
Individual	**Team**
Olympic Games silver medal, 400m medley (Moscow 1980)	European Championships bronze medal, 4 x 100m freestyle (Jonkoping 1977)
European Championships bronze medal, 400m medley (Jonkoping 1977)	Commonwealth Games silver medal, 4 x 100m freestyle (Edmonton 1978)
Commonwealth Games gold medal, 200m medley (Edmonton 1978)	Commonwealth Games silver medal, 4 x 200m freestyle (Auckland 1990)
Commonwealth Games gold medal, 400m medley (Edmonton 1978)	Commonwealth Games bronze medal, 4 x 100m medley (Edmonton 1978)
	Commonwealth Games bronze medal, 4 x 100m freestyle (Auckland 1990)

Appointed MBE in 1993

Honorary doctorate from Exeter University, 2010

NISHA DESAI

How I first became involved in sport

I became serious about athletics at school after our Sports Day in Year 5, when a local coach spotted me winning the 800m by a huge distance. He asked me to join his group and three months later I started training twice a week with him, and have not stopped running competitively since.

I had already been involved in various sports, including swimming, gymnastics and also the usual 'knockabouts' with my older brother and his friends, playing football and cricket ... even though the school teacher said girls weren't allowed to play on the school team, much to my dismay! I just loved sport and the competitiveness. I have my older brother to blame for turning me into a tomboy!

At school I played netball and hockey, playing for U18 county in the latter and continued both sports at university. There was just something about athletics though, that I loved.

Inspiration

When I first started competing, I was inspired by Liz McColgan. I loved watching her run and would sit for the whole duration of the London Marathon just to watch her on TV.

When I was at school, I was given Lillian Board's biography and to date this is one of my favourite and most inspirational reads. Despite what she went through, she kept fighting and this book taught me a lot about perseverance and determination. It was especially good timing for me, as I read it not long after I had a heart operation and was told not to run again. My stubbornness was never going to let that be an option!

My mum has also been a massive inspiration because she always says, 'Once you've started something you must finish it' and I applied this to all my races. The only DNF I have to my name is when I collapsed during an 800m with heart arrhythmias, even then I tried to get back up to finish the race!

Memories

When I was little, my brother and I used to play football in our driveway and he used to put me in goal so he had all the fun of scoring. However, I was too competitive and used to dive on the ground, despite it being concrete, just to avoid being beaten!

When I was 13, we were travelling to the Northern Cross-country Championships in Lincoln. It's a long journey from Northumberland on a good day, but was made longer by the snow! Despite the fact there were severe weather warnings all the way on the radio saying 'do not travel unless absolutely essential' we were not deterred. Of course the Northern Championships were 'essential'! Unfortunately when we got there, they had already cancelled the race deeming it too dangerous. Not sure dad was too pleased driving all that way!

What I am doing now

Athletics has been a part of my life for 26 years now and despite the tears, niggles, pain and braving the winter training, when I hate being cold, it has been worth it. It has taught me so much and I have been lucky to experience the elation of sport and having that escape from a full-time job as a clinical pharmacist! Despite still competing, I have started doing some coaching and look forward to many more years in the sport. 🔥

ACHIEVEMENTS

English Schools silver medal Senior Girls, 800m (2002)

UK U20 Indoor Champion, 800m

10-times Northern Senior Champion (8 x 400m hurdles, 1 x 400m & 1 x 800m)

UK Inter Counties, multiple medsalist 400m hurdles

England Senior Champs, multiple medalist 400m hurdles

British Universities, multiple medalist, 800m (Indoor & Outdoor)

Representing England at Manchester International (2017)

TABLE TENNIS

SOPHIE EARLEY

How I first became involved in sport

I was very active from a young age. I loved to climb and also play football in the playground. I got a taste for table tennis as young as six, and thought I could be quite good at it. I have two brothers, Zak and Thomas, who also play. I remember watching them at their senior school which was really into table tennis (I go there now too) and wanting to be that good. A coach came to the school, watched them play and invited them to go to his club. My brothers joined and really liked it, but I was only five at the time and he told me I'd have to wait until I was six, even though I was busting to get on to the table and play too! The coach ran another club so we went there as well and that's where I really started to play regularly.

Inspiration

I didn't watch videos or training films, as such. I preferred to watch the top players at my own club and see how good they were. That's what inspired me to train harder and improve and be like them. My mum started taking me away to tournaments. The first was in Guernsey – an Open Primary Schools event – and I came second in that one, and did best in the team. I quickly became fascinated by the different spins you can use and the different shots to play. In 2014 I moved to a different club, Ormeau TTC, and found it was better for me. The coaches there, Keith Knox and Gervis Knox, were really good and great motivators and suited my game particularly well. They reinforced what I was doing right rather than dwelling on what I was doing wrong and that worked best for me.

Memories

I'm still very young so these memories are quite limited. A lot of hard work springs to mind! I play every night: Monday, Tuesday, Thursday at my club and Wednesday squad training with Ulster at the Lisburn Rackets club; Friday & Saturday with my brothers at a Leisure Centre which has a table, and we play for a couple of hours. I also work out at home, and have fitness drills. I have to do these a few times each week. I actually have a fitness programme from the University of Ulster at Jordanstown to adhere to, with different exercises twice a week. Overall, I just enjoy winning and achieving what we call 'a podium place'.

A few years ago I was injured and had to go to a physiotherapist. The impact of the injury was extreme and I was very down. That was a hard time.

My brothers continue to be helpful and supportive. At Christmas in 2017 they saved up their money and gave it to my mother to buy me some special table tennis shoes, which cost nearly £100. They knew they were shoes I needed.

Both are delighted when I do well, and I feel the same way about them. They have both done their coaching badges and take Ulster sessions.

What I am doing now

I am still working hard and competing. I want to continue to establish myself, improve and enjoy the sport. When I compete in Europe in my age group, it's just me. There aren't really any other girls in NI who are my standard, unfortunately. Long term, I might want to make a living from the game and, if I can, win a medal at the Olympic Games. I now attend Malone College in Finaghy, which is very supportive. The Principal is encouraging, and helps me get school work to take away with me to competitions as I don't want to fall behind.

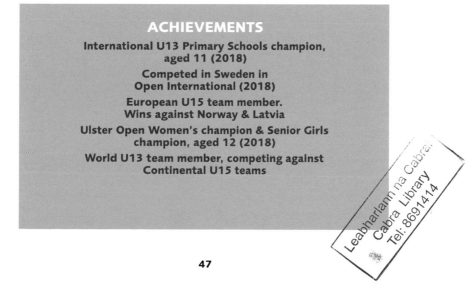

ACHIEVEMENTS

International U13 Primary Schools champion, aged 11 (2018)

Competed in Sweden in Open International (2018)

European U15 team member. Wins against Norway & Latvia

Ulster Open Women's champion & Senior Girls champion, aged 12 (2018)

World U13 team member, competing against Continental U15 teams

HEIDE ECKER-ROSENDAHL

How I first became involved in sport

When I was a small child, my father accepted a job as manager and director of a sports school, financed and controlled by the state sport federation. He and my mother managed the school for 25 years. Our family lived in a lovely flat overlooking an athletics field, and the entire area was not only beautiful but ideal for sports. At an early age I enjoyed running and jumping, not only on the track but in the forest right next to it. One of my first memories of athletic competition was during my second year in school. I was seven years old and won the class long jump competition with a leap of 3.71 meters, a metre further than anyone else.

Inspiration

My parents recognised the talent deep down inside me, but were hesitant to put too much pressure on me to train. Quite frankly, I've never been the type of person to react positively to that kind of pressure. Like any teenager I sometimes rebelled against the rules my parents set down for me. Nevertheless, I began training under my father's watchful eye when I was still a child and learned to love athletics despite our occasional differences of opinion. He was still active as a discus thrower at that time, and wildly mixed groups of young and old on the training field below our

flat were nothing unusual. Even at that time I realized that without doing sports in general, and without training in particular, I just would not have been happy. Luckily, I found an exceptional young athletics coach in my home town who accepted my strong personality. The young Gerd Osenberg turned into an internationally-known, world-class coach, and I worked with him with great pleasure and much success till the end of my career. I can also vividly remember a sports film that contributed to my early passion for athletic competition. It told the story of the 1960 Olympic decathlon in Rome. Rafer Johnson (USA) and C.K. Yang (Taiwan) were friends and students at the University of California in Los Angeles at that time, and trained together in preparation for the Olympic competition. Their battle for gold was absolutely thrilling for me.

Memories

The often-highlighted pentathlon competition at the Munich Olympics in 1972 was simply a joy to experience for me, and certainly a cherished memory in my life. In the previous five years before the Olympic games in Munich I had won all of the 15 pentathlon competitions that I had entered, but Burglinde Pollak from East Germany held the World record. In my heart I'd always been an all-rounder in athletics, someone who loved multi-event competition. I loved a good fight against worthy opponents, and both Burglinde and Mary Peters of Northern Island were world-class athletes.

The drama of the competition from my perspective began at the end of day one with the high jump. Back problems inherited from my mom forced me to use the straddle technique, and I ended up having to be satisfied with 1.65 meters. Mary, in comparison, set another personal best with 1.82m using the Fosbury Flop technique, and both she and Burglinde ended day one at the top of the field. I was in fifth place, 200 points behind Burglinde and 300 behind Mary. Without a doubt it was going to be exceptionally difficult to catch them. By the time the long jump competition was over on the morning of the second day, I had reduced their lead to 74 points for Burglinde and 121 points for Mary. My first jump that morning carried me 6.83m, one centimetre under my World record and I had proved to myself that I still had a chance to win. The last event in the pentathlon was the 200 metres. My time of 22.96 seconds was a German national record. I was far enough ahead of my two opponents to make the wait for the official announcement really exciting.

I was honestly pleased for Mary, whom I had known for a long time, that she had set personal bests in four of the five events and won the gold medal by 10 points. In fact, all three of the pentathlon medal winners that day broke the old World record. I was proud and happy to have been a part of the most exciting pentathlon competition of my career.

ACHIEVEMENTS

Olympic Games gold medals, Long Jump & 4 x 100m (Munich 1972)

Olympic Games silver medal, Pentathlon (Munich 1972)

European Games gold medal, Pentathlon (Helsinki 1971)

European Indoor Championhips gold medal, Pentathlon (Sofia 1971)

German Sportswoman of the Year, 1970 & 1972

What I am doing now

Like Mary, I have reached an age at which it makes sense to pass the torch to a younger generation. I continue to serve as a Vice-President of the Sports Foundation of our state government in North Rhine-Westphalia, an organisation which aids young athletes in our region. I also serve as the second chairperson for the Herman van Veen Foundation. Herman van Veen is a popular Dutch entertainer who cares passionately for needy children and the disabled. We have many projects to help children and families in need.

Perhaps my greatest joy and challenge at this stage in my life is my interaction with my four grandchildren. In moments of family play we can envision them as a new generation of Olympians, fighting for gold like Mary and I did so long ago. But even if our dreams don't come true, all our lives will have been touched by the spirit of the Olympics and my four grandchildren will be better human beings because of it. Even if they don't win Olympic medals, they won my heart long ago.

SAILING

TRACY EDWARDS MBE

How I first became involved in sport

I was expelled from school at the age of 15 and then fell out with my stepfather, so I went backpacking to get away from home. I began working on charter yachts in Greece when I was 17 and learned to sail and compete. So it was pure chance, some might say luck, that I got involved. Regardless, sailing gave me a second chance at life.

Inspiration

My mother and father inspired me. My mum was a champion rally driver and my father navigated. They worked in perfect harmony in every area of their lives until my father died when I was 10. They both told me that I could do anything I put my mind to, and that has stayed with me all my life.

Memories

When *Maiden* was in Uruguay for the leg stopover of the 1989/90 Whitbread Round the World race we were all invited to Susan Barrantes' polo ranch in Argentina for lunch. It was a buffet but with really small plates. As we had all just spent six weeks in the Southern Ocean, we kept going up for more and more food. We didn't notice that everyone else was waiting ... until a waiter whispered in my ear that the buffet selection was only the first course, and that they couldn't serve the main meal until we stopped eating! Awkward!

ACHIEVEMENTS

Whitbread Round the World Race, 2nd in class in *Maiden Great Britain* (1989/90)

Yachtsman of the Year Trophy, first ever woman winner in 32 years of award (1990)

Formed first all-female Multihull crew competing in Jules Verne Trophy for non-stop circumnavigation of the globe. Five World records before catamaran was dismasted (1998)

Formed first mixed gender team for *Maiden II*, breaking four major world records

Appointed MBE in 1990

Sportswoman of the Year, 1990

People of the Year Courage Award, 1995

Honorary Member, Lady Taverners

VERONA ELDER MBE

How I became involved in sport

My schoolteacher encouraged me.

Inspiration

Definitely Ann Packer when she ran the 800m for Great Britain. I liked to watch her on TV.

Memories

When I was competing for England or Great Britain, we were very close as a team. So much so, we used to bake cakes and take them with us on trips.

Bad diet ... great fun!

ACHIEVEMENTS

Individual

Commonwealth Games silver medal, 400m (Christchurch 1974)

Commonwealth Games silver medal, 400m (Edmonton 1978)

European Indoor Championships gold medal, 400m (1973, 1975, 1979)

European Indoor Championships silver medal, 400m (1977)

European Indoor Championships bronze medal, 400m (1981)

Team

Commonwealth Games gold medal, 4 x 400m (Christchurch 1974)

Commonwealth Games silver medal, 4 x 400m (Edmonton 1978)

Represented Great Britain 72 times

Appointed MBE in 1983

ATHLETICS

DAME JESSICA ENNIS-HILL DBE

How I first became involved in sport

I discovered athletics at a school holiday children's athletics event when I was 10. I was an active child and had tried other sports, including basketball, but once I tried athletics I stuck with it.

Inspiration

I had two female athletes – both heptathletes – that I looked up to at different stages of my career, Denise Lewis and later Carolina Kluft. My grandad was also a huge supporter of mine and helped enormously in the early years and my parents have been a constant source of encouragement throughout my career too.

Memories

Winning gold at the London Olympics in 2012 was just the most amazing moment and a huge relief too. To be in front of a home crowd with my whole family there was very special. I think then to win the 2015 World title in Beijing, with just 10 months of training under my belt after having my son Reggie, has got to be one of my proudest moments. It was totally unexpected and such a huge achievement.

My toughest time in my career was missing the 2008 Beijing Olympics with stress fractures in my foot. I was on a really positive trajectory with my career at the time, and to find myself with my foot in a cast a short time before the Games was very hard to deal with. Retrospectively, however, I think that winning in London was all the sweeter for it.

What I am doing now

I am working on a number of projects that motivate people to be more active – not at an elite level but for people everywhere. I am working hard on a fitness website and app to help women have fitter and healthier pregnancies and to encourage them to maintain healthier lifestyles before and after having their babies. I am also working on a project for higher education that will train students to be coaches and use sport to help them further their education and achieve a valuable qualification.

ACHIEVEMENTS

Olympic Games gold medal, heptathlon (London 2012)

Olympic Games silver medal, heptathlon (Rio 2016)

World Championships 3 x gold medals, heptathlon (Berlin 2009, Daegu 2011 & Beijing 2015)

World Indoor Champion, pentathlon (Doha 2010)

European Championships gold medal, heptathlon (Barcelona 2010)

British record holder for heptathlon – 6955 points

Appointed DBE in 2017

Appointed CBE in 2013

RUGGBY UNION

JUDO &
WEIGHTLIFTING

NON EVANS MBE

How I first became involved in sport

I was born with the umbilical cord wrapped around my head three times, and my mother claims I haven't stopped moving since. I could walk when I was eight months old and run before I was one. I used to pull my sister around the garden on her tricycle saying I wanted muscles, and I still have them 36 years later. I used to have her time me running laps around the garden – called interval training these days.

Inspiration

There were no real role models when I was young, but I loved rugby and used to watch Ieuan Evans who played for Llanelli & Wales, I wanted to be like him. Roger Federer is one of my favourite sports stars because he works hard and just gets on with it. No fuss, just pure hard work and talent.

ACHIEVEMENTS

Olympic Games, Freestyle Wrestling Champion (2010)

Commonwealth Games Judo silver medals (1994 & 1998)

Welsh weightlifting champion (2000–2002)

Welsh Judo Champion (1990–2002)

87 Rugby Union caps for Wales

64 tries for Wales, a World record

463 international points for Wales

Top points scorer in World & Welsh International Women's rugby

Appointed MBE in 2011

Inducted into the Welsh Sports Hall of Fame (2012)

Memories

Wales had never beaten England in 22 Years of trying. We were losing 15–13 and time was up. We had a penalty in injury time and there was no time to go for touch or scrum, so it was either tap-and-go or try to kick the goal. I was the kicker for the team and the captain asked me if I was happy to go for it. I said yes. Thankfully it went over ... and we won by 16 points to 15. It was a real David and Goliath battle as England players are professional and Wales amateur. It was my proudest moment. But I had not heard the final whistle. I was mobbed by the team and all I kept saying was 'Have we won? Have we won?' It was incredible. Wales have never beaten England since and I can't see it happening for another 22 years!

NICOLA FAIRBROTHER

How I first became involved in sport

My mum and dad took me and my brother Darren, when we were aged eight and seven respectively, to an Army Display in Aldershot, where we had a go at judo on a makeshift mat. Darren loved it and wanted to take it up, so I went along with him when he went to his first session at the Bracknell Judo Club and decided I would also give it a go. It seemed a better option than sitting and waiting on the side. It turned out that I loved the sport, but Darren didn't like it so much and gave it up about a year later.

Inspiration

Throughout my career I was inspired and motivated by my coach Don Werner, who seemed to know just the right words that needed to be said (or sometimes not said) when I was about to compete. At the time, the British Judo team was full of inspirational champions and, as a young International fighter, I would be able to train with multiple world champions like Karen Briggs, Loretta Cusack-Doyle, Ann Hughes, Sharon Rendle and Diane Bell. They inspired me greatly and showed me what was possible and, also very importantly at a technical level, how to achieve it.

Memories

I was standing on the mat, just about to go into the 1992 European final. My coach Don was by my side as I 'psyched up', and he said something along the lines of: 'Come on girlie, you can do this'. I remember I replied rather robotically, 'I'll do my best.'

> "No Nic, don't do your best. Do better than your best."

That's when Don stopped me jumping up and down, put an arm on my shoulder and said: 'No Nic, don't do your best. Do better than your best. When you think there is nothing more left in the bag there is always a little bit more if you dig deep for it. Do better than your best'.

I went on to win this final – my first European gold medal of three. Don Werner had the ability to bring out the best in all his pupils, to make them do more than they thought was possible.

ACHIEVEMENTS

Individual

Olympic Games silver medal, lightweight (Barcelona 1992)

Olympic Games 5th place (Atlanta 1996)

World Champion (Hamilton, Canada 1993)

European Champion (1992, 1993 & 1995)

British Champion nine times

RACHEL FENWICK

How I first became involved in sport

The local council in Co. Longford, Ireland, where I lived as a child, built a wall for anyone to hit a tennis ball against. I did this for hours on end. I loved my sport at school where I played hockey and tennis and dabbled in athletics. However, I never learned to swim because there was only a canal at the end of the garden and the water was not very clean. Later, when I joined the WRAF, sport was a very high priority and the facilities were excellent.

My late husband Roy was in the RAF for 12 years and, when we were stationed in Hong Kong, he discovered an archery club. He seemed to spend all his spare time either shooting or looking after his equipment. I was saving up our money to buy something like a standard lamp, but each time I nearly had enough he would 'need' another set of arrows, which, of course, had to come from the USA. I wasn't keen on archery at that time!

Returning to Berkshire in the UK, Roy found another club and I went with him one Sunday afternoon. While the members shot, I tried to keep our two children safe from the arrows. Eventually, when tea was served, I was persuaded to have a go. I actually hit the target and was instantly smitten. All our spare time between shifts was spent at the club … and we ate packed salads.

Appearing in *Midsomer Murders*

56

ACHIEVEMENTS

Individual

**Olympic Games, represented GB
(Montreal 1976)**

**One World Championship & three
European Championships**

Team

**World Championships bronze medal
(Berlin 1979)**

Multiple National Championship wins

I didn't drive, so I would put all my equipment on my bicycle to head off and shoot up to 144 arrows a day. What with doing shift work, and running a home and family, it was hard work. I was selected to represent the county, then chosen for an overseas trip to Italy where I beat some of the established ladies in the GB team. I was chosen for the Olympic Games in 1976, at the age of 41.

Inspiration

Maeve Kyle, the Irish Olympian who taught us hockey at school, had a great influence on me. Later, I was inspired by watching Ann Packer, Mary Rand, Lillian Board and Mary Peters. I am still inspired by athletes of all abilities.

Memories

I formed my own archery club in Somerset, where I helped teach a blind lady. She said that being able to shoot with sighted and able-bodied people – and be treated in the same way – was like having Christmas every day. That made me feel really good.

I remember at one shoot the fastening on my bra broke. A friend offered to repair it with a safety pin but when I was at full draw with the bow, the pin opened and stuck in my backbone. I remember thinking: 'Do I release the arrow or come down and start again?' Either way, it was painful.

At an event in Worcestershire, the toilet facilities were so basic the ladies had to pass through the back of the gents to get to their cubicles. Discretion required us to wait until we could hear no voices before coming out again. I had to wait for so long, I nearly missed the start of my event.

DONNA FRASER

How I first became involved in sport

I loved running and apparently ran everywhere as a child. My older sister loved athletics, so I was exposed to it at a very early age, as there's a 10-year age gap. I enjoyed PE at school, although the thought of wearing vest and knickers really didn't appeal, to be honest! My first race was representing my primary school at the age of eight at the Croydon Schools, where I ran 55m. I was so nervous.

Inspiration

My first inspiration was my sister. I would stuff her spikes with tissue (because they were way too big for me) when she was at school and run in the garden. She supported me throughout my career and drove me miles around the country to compete. The more my love for athletics grew, the more I was inspired by Jesse Owens and Wilma Rudolph, both of whom achieved so much despite adversity, which I admire enormously!

My late coach, Ayo Falola, took me to the next level in my career and inspired me to be the best I could be.

Memories

Athletics was and is my life. My first fond memory was winning the European Junior Championships in 1991. No one expected me to even make the final. It was a great feeling seeing the GB flags in the

ACHIEVEMENTS

Olympic Games finalist, fourth 400m (Sydney 2000)

Commonwealth Games triple medallist (Kuala Lumpur 1998)

crowd going crazy when I finished. By contrast, of course, there have always been 'down' times with injuries.

At my first Olympic Games in Atlanta (1996), I was sharing an apartment with seven other girls who are still my girlfriends to this day – Denise Lewis, Marcia Bailey (née Richardson), Jacqui Agyepong, Michelle Robinson (née Griffith), Stephanie Douglas, Simmone Jacobs and Geraldine McLeod. Being the baby of the group, they were like my big sisters and showed me the ropes. When I was told we had to have a gender test, they teased me and said I needed to strip off completely and get checked. I was absolutely mortified and petrified at the same time. When I arrived at the centre, all it turned out to be was a saliva swab. The relief was unbelievable, clearly the girls' way of initiating me into the group.

What I am doing now

I am Vice President and Equality, Diversity and Engagement Lead for UK Athletics. I have my fingers in many other pies, including being a member of the Sport Honours Committee, Trustee for the Women's Sport Trust and the London Marathon Charitable Trust.

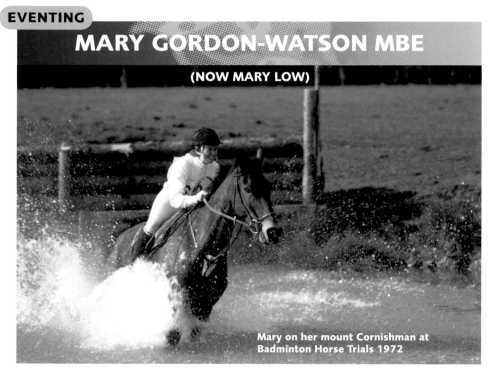

EVENTING

MARY GORDON-WATSON MBE
(NOW MARY LOW)

Mary on her mount Cornishman at Badminton Horse Trials 1972

Inspiration

My mother was my inspiration from an early age, driving the family around to Pony Club, and onwards. She made it possible and always encouraged us. I was the keenest and most competitive of my family, but we all rode. She also arranged for Sergeant Ben Jones to teach me during his holiday, and he became my main inspiration, as an adult competitor. Ben went on to ride at the Tokyo Olympics, and won a gold medal at the Mexico Olympics. He was generous with his time, and taught me important basics that were a foundation for later success in eventing. Sadly, he died young in the 1970s. I built a partnership with my father's horse, Cornishman, who was a truly great horse that provided all the necessary incentive, to do justice to his talents.

ACHIEVEMENTS

Olympic Games team gold medal
(Munich 1972)

World Champion (Ireland 1970)

World Championships gold medals
(Ireland 1970 & England 1971)

European Champion (France 1969)

Sportswoman of the Year, 1970

DAME KATHERINE GRAINGER DBE

How I first became involved in sport

My big sister Sarah was one school year above me and so generally had to put up with my tagging along to everything ... swimming, badminton, netball, karate, squash, running, cycling and hockey. We were both, and still remain, fiercely competitive!

Inspiration

Because of our competitive streak, my sister was probably my first inspiration. However, I had great PE teachers at school and my art teacher taught karate and showed me how very high levels of competition and participation can also be fun and friendly.

Bruce Lee was an incredible philosopher as well as an athlete and his style of thinking beyond just the obvious was very influential. He understood the power of the mind and the ability of the human body to do incredible things.

When I started rowing we had some of the best athletes in the world within the British team. Steve Redgrave and Matthew Pinsent were setting standards and breaking records and I consider myself incredibly lucky to have my sporting career overlap with theirs. Sydney 2000 was my first Olympic games and Steve's last, and witnessing how he, his crew and his coach approached that historic race was a masterclass in delivering the right performance in a high pressure situation.

Memories

Talking of pressure, Sydney was also where I watched Cathy Freeman, the Australian 400m runner, light the Olympic Cauldron in the Opening Ceremony and I was back in the stadium to witness her memorable 400m final. It felt the entire stadium held their breath as she approached the start line, and

Katherine with her 2012 Olympic Gold medal

then erupted in the most deafening and blinding display of sound and light as cheering and flashbulbs dominated the stadium. Cathy made history that day when she became the Olympic Champion and it was such a privilege, and inspiration, to be there to see it.

My more painful memories are inevitably the disappointments. Beijing 2008 was probably the lowest point of my career, partly because – although I was in a crew that won a silver medal – for the four years building up to that Olympic final we had solely focused on winning gold. Silver felt like failure and it took a long time to come to terms with it. The proudest aspect of the aftermath, as a crew and as a wider group, including our coach and wonderful support team, was that there was no blame, no finger-pointing afterwards. Everyone accepted her own responsibility. A real test of a team is when things go wrong and I think, as painful as that time was, we coped well and supported each other.

What I am doing now

The most obvious and visible things that athletes leave sport with is an array of results, medals, and records. The more intangible but, I believe, more valuable thing you leave with is a collection of memories, experiences, and friendships that last long after the trophies fade and the records are broken. When I left competition behind me I thought that I had also lost the incredible camaraderie that sport brings, the wonderful, uniting sense of being on a mission together, caring and challenging each other, problem-solving and dreaming together. Happily, I am now the Chair of UK Sport and have found there a very similar environment. It's a world full of dedicated, focused, committed individuals who care passionately about what they do and strive every day to make a positive difference to the high performance system. They tackle huge challenges with a healthy sense of humour and a spirit of resilience. It's a wonderful step out of the part of sport I knew and cherished into a different part of sport. I love it and I still feel inspired by it every day.

ACHIEVEMENTS

Olympic Games, medals at five consecutive games, gold (London 2012) & silver (Rio 2016, Beijing 2008, Athens 2004, & Sydney 2000)

World Championships, 6 gold medals (2003–2011)

Appointed DBE in 2017

Appointed CBE in 2013

Appointed MBE in 2006

Chancellor of Oxford Brookes University

WATER SKIING

JANET GRAY MBE

How I first became involved in sport

Swimming and life-saving were my sports as a child, I just loved anything water-based. I should stress at the outset that I was sighted throughout my school years and there was little hint of a hereditary condition that would ultimately cost me my sight. My father developed a very rare eye disease and was totally blind by the time I was five years old, but there was no trace of it in other members of the family. My vision wasn't perfect, so like many people, I wore glasses and then contact lenses, but I was able to drive when I was old enough and passed my test at 17. I also played hockey and netball at school but I was absolutely useless at anything racket-based. LOL. I couldn't hit anything like a tennis ball or shuttlecock as I didn't have good hand-eye coordination, but I enjoyed all sport and if you put me in water I was in my element.

Inspiration

I went to Greymount Girls School in Belfast, where Mrs Morrison and Mrs Erskine took us for sport. They made everything fun as well as competitive, and that was encouraging. I met my husband Paul when I was 17, and Paul was a water skier, but was out of his sport due to an injury. I lost my sight at 21 and we were married shortly afterwards. Paul's Uncle Jimmy was visiting us one day and suggested that Paul should return to his sport, so the following weekend, Paul and I went to the lake. I sat in the boat while Paul skied and thought it was very exciting. Then, out of the blue, they asked me if I wanted to have a go! I agreed immediately, as prior to losing my sight, I was a Life-Saving Teacher and Swimming Instructor and had no fear in water. Uncle Jimmy drove the boat and Paul went out alongside me on a second rope and told me when to stand up. I got up first time and we did three laps of the lake and I found it absolutely exhilarating. I loved the speed and the rush, and soon wondered if I could go out and do this on my own. When they said they thought I could, I was hooked. Paul and I joined a water ski club together. I went to the Irish Nationals in 1996, qualified for the Europeans the following year and went off to Denmark and won a silver and bronze medal. I was just doing slalom tricks at that time as I hadn't learnt to jump competitively. I qualified for the World Championships in America two weeks later and won a bronze medal. It all happened very quickly for me. I went to Jordan in the Middle East in 1998 and I won silver and bronze medals again and won the World Disabled Water Ski Championships for the first time in 1999, then 2001, 2003 and 2007. →

ACHIEVEMENTS

16 world championship gold medals
World record holder in slalom, tricks & jump

Appointed MBE in 2002
Awarded an honorary doctorate from Queen's University, Belfast, 2004
Given the Freedom of the City of Lisburn, 2009

Memories

It would be remiss of me not to mention the traumatic life-changing incident and the injuries I suffered, which help define many of my subsequent achievements.

I used to live three months of each winter in Florida, warm-weather training, and it was in March of 2004 while I was training at water ski school in Tampa, that I suffered a traumatic accident. I left the dock behind the boat, on what should have been just a routine training exercise around the lake on a pair of brand new jump skis, when suddenly and without warning, there was a massive impact, as I was whipped at high speed into the back-end of the large metal jump ramp in the middle of the lake! It wasn't good ... I was air-lifted to the Tampa General Hospital. I had sustained multiple injuries and was on life-support! I died four times in intensive care, but was resuscitated. The specialists said that if I survived, I would never walk again, and even advised Paul to plan my funeral! Thankfully, I defied all the odds. I had 44 operations over 12 years, which only finished in 2016, and worked incredibly hard to get my life back together. As far as I was concerned, surviving was the first step ... the next step was to become independent again. I was damned if I was going to be completely blind *and* in a wheelchair *and* totally dependent on others for the rest of my life! I managed to block out all the pain and I am happy to talk about it now I've come through it. Initially I had

long metal rods in my leg and hip holding things together but this meant I had lost a lot of feeling in one leg and eventually persuaded the surgeon to remove the rods even though it was an 18-month recovery period from that operation alone.

In 2006 Mary Peters and I went away to Manchester for a weekend and we were staying with friends just a couple of miles from where my Team GBNI coach was based. He hadn't seen me since before my accident so I managed to persuade Mary to go and see him before we flew home. Mary had

64

gone off for a walk, and my coach casually asked if I would like to try to ski again. He immediately left the room and came back with a wetsuit and towel and simply told me to hurry up! I was putting the wetsuit on when Mary returned from a walk and honestly, I thought she was going to kill me. She knew what I was planning to do and told me I couldn't take the risk so soon after surgery, but I needed to know if I would be able to ski again. I just tootled behind the boat and took it very gently but I did manage to get up on the ski first time. I was the happiest girl.

My doctor was furious at the risk I had taken and I know I could have done a lot more damage. It took a few more months of recuperation before I tried again. I'm not a very patient patient, and not very sensible and self-aware when challenges are put in front of me. I have legacies from the accident and this will continue, but I manage them. The wonderful medical experts put me back together over 12 years, and eventually I improved enough to go back to the World Championships again in Australia with Team GBNI!

The home country and America both had full teams of 14 skiers but we could only afford to take seven. If we were going to hold on to the world team title we all had to produce tremendous performances ... but we managed to do it, reigning victorious and I regained all my titles, bringing five gold medals home! I was the only Northern Ireland representative in the team.

What I am doing now

I retired at the end of 2012 and had to think long and hard about what I was going to do next. I enjoy motivational speaking, but knew that with the downturn in the economy, I wasn't going to make a living out of it in NI. To my surprise a friend and local MLA, Edwin Poots, came to see me and asked if I had considered standing for the council. I hadn't the first notion about politics but as a Freeman of the City of Lisburn I thought it would be a lovely way to give something back.

Opportunity doesn't knock very often, especially when you are a woman heading towards 50 and ... blind, to boot! LOL. I've learnt through life that you've got to grasp every opportunity when it comes your way. Give it your best shot. If it doesn't work out at least you've had a go. Coming from my background of sport and the charity voluntary sector I knew I had the skill set. I was delighted to get over the line and be selected. I was their first blind councillor – they've learnt a lot from me and I've learnt a lot from them.

There was a lot to discover about the workings of the council and the protocols but I enjoyed the work. There aren't many advantages to being blind but sometimes it opens doors and you can achieve things that might not otherwise have been possible. People don't like to backpedal, or say 'no' to me, so I get things done. As an athlete you're always striving for the top – and that applies to politics, or whatever else you do in life outside of sport.

LOUISE GREER BEM

PARALYMPIC EQUESTRIANISM

How I first became involved in sport

I was diagnosed with meningitis at the age of two, and was fortunate to survive. However, I had to have both my legs amputated and part of one arm. Ultimately, horse riding was my physiotherapy. I was asked if there was something I would like to do, that I had always wanted to do before I was disabled, and I replied, 'horse riding'. My physiotherapist agreed that it would help develop my core strength, and my ability to walk in prosthetic legs. By the age of 10 I was doing everything by myself. I joined Riding for the Disabled and didn't really look back.

Inspiration

Lee Person, a Paralympic gold medallist on the GB team.

Memories

I don't really remember anything about my illness, being in hospital or my operations because I was so young. So my memories are all based on the way I am. I haven't known any different, it's normal to me. If people don't realize, and ask me if I am suffering from an injury, I simply tell them, 'No, I've got no legs!' I feel that I can do anything when I'm riding. I can jump and I can run through fields. My horse allows me to do everything that I can't. She is my legs. I never wish I hadn't become ill. If I

ACHIEVEMENTS

Member of the Irish Paralympic Squad for dressage

Competitor, RDA National Championships (two classes)

Degree in Equine Business Management from Hartpury College

Awarded BEM in 2015

hadn't had meningitis, I wouldn't be the person I am nor have had the opportunity to do everything I've been able to do.

I was amazed when I received the letter telling me I had received the BEM. I even had a sculpture made of me for the Chelsea Flower Show!

I do recall going out on my horse 'Tizer' for our daily training, and he took off in a canter and went over a jump. I managed to stay on over the jump, but once we landed I fell off – with my arm still attached to the reins. The children and I were laughing, their parents not so much. They thought my arm had been dislocated.

What I am doing now

I am in the Irish Paralympic squad for dressage and would love to be in Tokyo in 2020. I also campaign and raise awareness for Meningitis Now, which involves travelling around schools telling children, teachers and parents about what symptoms to watch for. I also work at Kemberton Riding Stables in Shropshire as a finance and advertising manager.

BARONESS GREY-THOMPSON DBE

How I first became involved in sport

I first became involved in sport when I was quite young. I swam and went horse riding among other things. My parents thought it was important that I was fit and strong to be able to move my wheelchair around and live independently. I was 12 when I started playing sport more seriously, and started doing some wheelchair racing in 1982. I just knew that I loved it more than any other activity and that it was what I wanted to do. My parents still encouraged me to play lots of sports and not concentrate on one too early, but at the age of 16 I began to focus on the racing.

Inspiration

There was a Welsh wheelchair athlete called Chris Hallam, who I remember watching compete in the London Marathon in the early 1980s and thinking that it was what I really wanted to do. I remember telling my mum that I was going to do the London Marathon one day and about five years later I was on the start line. Chris became a good friend and someone to look up to in many ways. He was a really professional athlete who had strong opinions in many areas, and he was also great fun to be around. ⇒

ACHIEVEMENTS

Paralympic Games gold medals, 100m 200m 400m & 800m (Barcelona 1992)

Paralympic Games gold medal, 800m (Atlanta 1996)

Paralympic Games gold medals, 100m 200m 400m & 800m (Sydney 2000)

Paralympic Games gold medals, 100m & 400m (Athens 2004)

Paralympic Games silver medal 4 x 100m (Barcelona 1992)

Paralympic Games silver medals, 100m 200m & 400m (Atlanta 1992)

Paralympic Games bronze medal, 400m (Seoul 1988)

World Championship gold medal, 200m (Birmingham 1998)

World Championship gold medal, 200m (Assen 2006)

World Championship silver medals, 400m & 800m (Birmingham 1998)

World Championship silver medal, 800m (Assen 2006)

World Championship bronze medal, 400m (Assen 2006)

Six London Marathon wins (Between 1992–2002)

30 World records during her career

Created a Life Peer in March 2010

Appointed DBE in 2005

Appointed OBE in 2000

Appointed MBE in 1993

Memories

Being at the Commonwealth Games in 2006 was one of my fondest memories. I knew that I was just about at the end of my career and I remember feeling at peace that I had gone as far as I could. I competed for Wales and was team captain, which was a huge privilege. I also got to carry the flag at the opening ceremony, which was incredibly emotional.

Trying to be a good mum is one of the hardest things that I have done, because your child doesn't come with a manual to tell you how it is meant to work. My daughter is an incredible young woman but I just try to give her opportunities to try different things, to see what she enjoys. I am away from home quite a lot and that makes it hard on the family.

Probably my best race was winning the 100m in Athens. It would have been considered my weakest event so to come through was one of the technically most perfect races that I have done, and it feels like I can remember every single push of the race.

Way back in Barcelona one of the wheelchair racing squad suggested that the true test of a British team member was the person who could eat the most ice cream (which was provided free in the village). I managed to eat three, which was the lowest number of anyone who took part. I can't remember what the winner ate (a lot!) but it showed the camaraderie in the team. I do remember feeling a bit sick at the end of it, but we had a couple of hours with each other at the end of the Games, where we just sat and spent time together, and I loved it.

What I am doing now

I enjoy watching wheelchair racing, and seeing young athletes come through the system. I am still involved in sport from a parliamentary perspective. I finished a piece of work for the Government for Duty of Care in Sport. It had a huge remit, but I am pleased with what I was able to do. What I would like to see is a Duty of Care applied to all those who are involved in sport because there are so many positive things that come from being involved in it.

ATHLETICS

SALLY GUNNELL OBE

How I first became involved in sport

I joined an athletics club when I was 12, after being encouraged by my PE teacher.

Inspiration

Daley Thompson's gold medal-winning decathlon in Moscow, 1980, was a huge inspiration. I couldn't believe that his coach at the time, Bruce Longden, asked me at the age of 14 to join his multi-event group. I loved Daley's cheekiness, yet ability to perform when it really mattered and particularly the Olympic battle he had with the German athlete, Jürgen Hingsen.

There was also the excitement I felt at watching Friday night athletics events at Crystal Palace, with the stadium packed under the bright lights, and watching Seb Coe and Steve Ovett run.

Then there was Shirley Strong, who was queen of the 100m hurdles, which was fast becoming my favourite event. I was often in awe of her skill and personality. She went on to win a silver medal at the Los Angeles Olympics. I started to get close to her in a competition, which felt really weird, and I had a real drive to win and beat her.

As I moved up to 400 hurdles, Ed Moses was the ultimate perfectionist and I spent many a day watching his races. I really wanted to get close to the domination of the event as he had done.

Memories

My fondest memories have to be some of the Commonwealth Games in Auckland and Victoria. It was so nice to compete and win. But just to look around and enjoy the whole event and the place was such fun with the rest of the girls.

The most painful memory was being carried off the track in the Atlanta Olympics. As reigning Olympic champ I didn't want to finish my career with a torn Achilles tendon and being carried off the track.

The first time I was invited to Buckingham Palace after winning my gold medals. I thought I was going to a large banquet. But it turned out to be a small dinner with just 12 people – the Queen, Nigel Mansell, a couple of actors – and the Duke of Edinburgh, whom I sat next to. My first dilemma was that I was wearing a rather large hat ... Her Majesty didn't. I was the only other woman so I wondered if I should leave it on or take it off, and if I did take it off where would I put it? I decided to leave it on. Then we had to be served the vegetables by the waiter from a very beautifully-presented dish with peas on one side and carrots the other and duchesse potatoes, which were there just to divide them. I was busy chatting to the Duke (as you do) and I scooped a spoonful of the potatoes which made the peas run into the carrots. You should have seen the look the waiter gave me. I had ruined his beautiful dish, and he still had to serve everyone else!

What I am doing now

My husband Jon is a coach to many top middle-distance athletes and I am still involved in the coaching and advising of the group. Our own son is part of the group, running 800m.

ACHIEVEMENTS

Individual

Olympic Games gold medal, 400m hurdles (Barcelona 1992)

World Championships gold medal & World record (Stuttgart 1993)

World Championships silver medal, 400m hurdle (Tokyo 1991)

European Championships, 4 gold medals in 400m hurdles (Rome 1993), (Birmingham 1994), (Madrid 1991), (Munich 1997)

Commonwealth Games, 3 x gold medals: 100m hurdles (Edinburgh 1986), 400m hurdles (1990 Auckland), 400m hurdles (Victoria 1994)

No other woman has held Commonwealth, European, World & Olympic track titles concurrently & although Sally's World record has been broken, her Stuttgart time remains a British record.

Team

Olympic Games bronze medal, 4 x 400m relay (Barcelona 1992)

Olympic Games bronze medal, 4 x 400m relay (Stuttgart 1993)

European Championships bronze medal, 4 x 400m relay (Split 1990)

Commonwealth Games, 2 x gold medals: 4 x 400m relay (Auckland 1990), (Victoria 1994)

Appointed OBE in 1998

Appointed MBE in 1993

Appointed Deputy Lieutenant of West Sussex in 2011

ARCHERY

SYLVIA HARRIS

How I first became involved in sport

Sport was just a natural progression of play as a child. However, my involvement in archery first started by accident, through a playmate who lived across the road from me. A club had been formed by a teacher at the local secondary school, Richard Wales, and through him I got a chance to try out archery. Participation always felt worthwhile and meaningful – later for its own sake and as a learning experience – even in search of the elusive 'high performance'. So my involvement continued.

Inspiration

I first felt inspired by the young Romanian gymnast, Nadia Comaneci, whom I saw on television in 1976. Hers was an incredible performance, with poise, precision and balance. I loved the fluidity, the grace, the power and her unbelievable skill level, apparently mixed with effortless action and some enjoyment too! It was freedom beyond discipline. How could somebody move so accurately in such a way? And it was all completed with arms outstretched, whole body of energy passing through to fingertips, a spine of stored energy bent backwards like a bow.

Inevitably, Nadia scored perfect 10s

not achieved in judged Olympic competition before. It was, perhaps, the nearest embodiment of movement and perfection humanly possible that I had ever seen. To me 10 was also a significant number in my own sport. At that same Olympic Games I first heard about archer Darrell Pace, who had the world at his feet.

Eight years later, and nine years after commencing my own journey, I made reserve for the British Olympic Team in the quieter and less outwardly dynamic sport of archery. Yes, I was disappointed at being a reserve, but undeterred.

A further eight years passed until I made my own Olympic debut. There was no medal and no perfection, but at least a sense of pride and further inspiration that has stayed somewhere deep inside me ever since.

What I am doing now

As long as I still have a body, my own longing is still to experience some freedom, flow and even the edge of perfection in my own way. If I can get close, even just to keep striving to be more than I currently am, for a little self mastery and everyday balance, that's good enough for me … .

ACHIEVEMENTS
GB Olympic team (Barcelona 1992)

CRICKET

BARONESS HEYHOE FLINT OBE

How I first became involved in sport

Both my parents were Physical Education teachers. My father played amateur football for Denmark where he trained as a PE Teacher. My mother played county tennis and hockey, and taught music and movement. It was their huge encouragement and investment (no grants or travelling expenses in those days) which steered me along the pathway to international sport.

Inspiration

I went to Wolverhampton Girls High School where hockey and cricket were the two main sports, and our PE teacher (herself a county cricket and hockey player) encouraged us to join local sports clubs to further our interests.

Memories

I learned a lot of cricket playing 'Test matches' in our garden with my brother Nicholas and his friends when I was about 10 years old.

The boys would not let me bat for three years – well I was only a girl! So when eventually I was allowed to bat, the boys couldn't get me out for three days. In the end they abandoned the cricket and decided, in the middle of June, that it was the football season!

You see a woman can never succeed in a man's world – hence my persistence in life to put women's cricket on the map, despite so much male opposition along the way from sponsors and sports editors.

ACHIEVEMENTS

Captain of England Women's Cricket team, 11 years undefeated

Member of England cricket team (1960–1981)

England Hockey international goalkeeper (1963–64)

First Honorary Lady Member of the MCC (1998) after fighting a nine-year battle to enable women to apply for membership. The MCC is the world cricket authority based at Lord's Cricket Ground, & had been an all-male club – 18,000 men, no women – since 1787.

Raised the profile of women's cricket by creating the first-ever World Cup of Cricket in 1973 (two years before the men's inaugural World Cup in 1975) & found sponsorship & patronage for England Women's cricket from Sir Jack Hayward (also, Wolverhampton-born).

Ennobled Baroness in 2010
Appointed OBE in 2008
Appointed MBE in 1972
Inducted into the ICC Cricket Hall of Fame, 2010 (the first woman to achieve this accolade)

Baroness Heyhoe Flint sadly passed away in January, 2017

KATE HOEY MP

FORMER SPORTS MINISTER

How I first became involved in sport

Being brought up on a small family farm I was always outside climbing trees and jumping ditches. At my grammar school, Belfast Royal Academy, I loved all sport and had some inspirational teachers. From the age of 13 I wanted to become a PE teacher myself and had a very happy 3 years qualifying at the Ulster College of Physical Education. I was once Northern Ireland high jump champion, but it could have been a different story. Mary Peters was injured at the time and didn't compete!

Inspiration

My earliest individual moment of inspiration was listening on the wireless to the world record-breaking run by Derek Ibbotson in the mile in 1957. It seemed such an amazing time. My cousin Madge Williamson, who was a PE teacher, taught me to swim and at college I was lucky enough to have Thelma Hopkins – former world high jump record-holder – in the year ahead of me. My parents were inspirational to me as they worked so hard in order to give my sister and brother and myself a wonderful start. I also was greatly encouraged by the Principal of the Ulster College of Physical Education, Oonah Pim, who was far ahead of the times in seeing that women could achieve so much.

Memories

As Sports Minister, I twice sat next to my Australian counterpart at the Sydney Olympics in 2000, and on each occasion the British won gold – first in shooting (Richard Faulds) and then in rowing (our wonderful four, led by Sir Steve Redgrave). Fearing my proximity was jinxing the Australian competitors, the minister refused to sit with me at the next event. However, we remain good friends. My fondest memory is being the first Sports Minister to attend the Isle of Man TT and garlanding Joey Dunlop as he won for the last time at this exciting motorcycle race. Just a few weeks later he was killed in Estonia and the whole of Northern Ireland mourned.

Sport has been so much part of my life and it will always be. The many fond memories will keep me busy in my old age.

Kate Hoey with Joey Dunlop

ACHIEVEMENTS

Before being elected as an MP I was Educational advisor to Arsenal FC (1985–89) and worked with the amazing youth team who went on to be the core group in the Arsenal League winning team of 1989. Appointed as the UK's first woman Sports Minister by the then Prime Minister Tony Blair in 1999. Appointed by the Mayor of London (now Prime Minister) Boris Johnson as his Sports Commissioner and worked to promote and increase funding to grassroots sport in London.

ATHLETICS
DAME KELLY HOLMES DBE

How I first became involved in sport

I wasn't academic at all and spent most of my time outside the classroom rather than in it. I felt I didn't get encouragement from most of my teachers, so I switched off. However, I started athletics at secondary school, and became more involved when my PE teacher, Debbie Page, came to me and said: 'Come on Kelly, you've got to start concentrating on something!' When she said I could be good at something, I listened. I began to beat all the girls who were two years above me – on a grass track that went up a hill. She called my mum and asked her to take me down to the local athletics club. There I met my first coach, Dave Arnold. Within six months of starting I was English Schools Champion, Kent Champion and National Champion at 1500m, and things went on from there. Sport made me feel good about myself and put me on a level playing field when I went back to school because suddenly I was someone, rather than the nobody in the corner.

Inspiration

At Olympic level it was Sebastian (now Lord) Coe, mainly because he was a 1500m and 800m runner. Because I wasn't doing athletics seriously in 1980, when I was 10, I wasn't really into the Olympic movement, even though I knew who he was. However, four years later when I was 14, I watched him win his gold medal in the 1500m and got goose bumps that day. I remember going back into school and telling my friends, who are still my best friends to this day, that I was going to be an Olympic champion.

Memories

When I went to my first Commonwealth Games in Victoria, Canada, in 1994, I was sharing an apartment with Sally Gunnell. She had won the World Championship and broken the World record in 1993, was Olympic Champion from 1992, and there I was, a newbie, rooming with her along with some other girls, which was quite overwhelming. I remember her coming out of the bathroom, and telling us all that she had just had a cold shower. I don't do cold showers, or just-warm showers for that matter, so I felt confident enough to ask her why she was doing it It was before ice baths became commonplace in sport, and she said it helped relax her legs. She then went on to win the gold medal for the 400m hurdles. That was good enough for me, so I thought I'd try one – not full body, but freezing water on my legs. I remember thinking, quite quickly: 'This doesn't b****y work,' and the other girls were laughing because they could hear me squealing. But I went out and won the 1500m.

"Come on Kelly, you've got to start concentrating on something!"

ACHIEVEMENTS

Olympic Games gold medals, 800m & 1500m (Athens 2004)

Olympic Games bronze medal, 800m (Sydney 2000)

World Championships, silver medal, 800m (Paris 2003)

World Championships silver medal, 1500m & bronze, 800m (Gothenburg 1995)

European Championships silver medal, 1500m (Helsinki 1994)

European Championships bronze medal, 800m (Munich 2002)

Commonwealth Games gold medals, 1500m (Victoria 1994 & Manchester 2002)

Commonwealth Games silver medal, 1500m (Kuala Lumpur 1998)

World Indoor Championships silver medal, 1500m (Birmingham 2003)

Appointed DBE in 2005

Appointed MBE (Military Division) in 1998

Honorary Colonel of the Royal Armoured Corps Training Regiment, 2018

Inducted into the England Athletics Hall of Fame, 2010

BBC Sports Personality of the Year, 2004

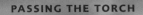

CYCLING

WENDY HOUVENAGHEL

How I first became involved in sport

I was always involved in sport throughout my school years, mostly participating in horse-riding, athletics and hockey. I also enjoyed participating in sport because it was beneficial to leading a healthy lifestyle. Later I could accompany my husband on cycle-training rides, so we spent a lot of time together cycling and taking part in competitions.

Inspiration

There are many sports people that have inspired me throughout my life in a whole variety of different sports, ranging from three-day eventing, show jumping, athletics and cycling. My husband and parents are the people whom I thought of the most whilst training and competing.

What I am doing now

I now participate in trail-running and have completed two ultra-marathons within the last year! I'm no longer involved with professional sport and am currently enjoying working as a dentist in Cornwall. I recently completed an implants course at Cambridge University and thoroughly enjoy running with my two large dogs!

ACHIEVEMENTS

Olympic Games silver medal, Women's Individual Pursuit (Beijing 2008)

World Championships silver medal, Women's Individual Pursuit (Poland 2009)

World Championships silver medal, Women's Individual Pursuit (Copenhagen 2010)

World Championships silver medal, Women's Individual Pursuit (Melbourne 2012)

Commonwealth Games silver medal, Women's Individual Pursuit (Delhi 2010)

World Championships gold medal, Women's Team Pursuit (Manchester 2008)

World Championships gold medal, Women's Team Pursuit (Poland 2009)

World Championships silver medal, Women's Team Pursuit (Copenhagen 2010)

European Championships gold medal, Women's Team Pursuit (Poland 2010)

World Championships gold medal, Women's Team Pursuit (Holland 2011)

UCI World Number 1 Ranking – Women's Team Pursuit – 2011

British National Individual Pursuit Champion (2005, 2006, 2010)

British National Circuit Time Trial Champion (2003, 2007, 2011 & 2012)

UCI World Number 1 Ranking, Women's Individual Pursuit (2006, 2007 & 2010)

ATHLETICS
CHERIECE HYLTON

How I first became involved in sport

I used to be a dancer before I became an athlete. From the age of two, I did ballet and tap which progressed into contemporary dance and acrobatics. Eventually I was performing in pantomimes with the likes of David Tennant and Rochelle Humes.

Inspiration

My parents inspired me. They didn't come from much, but showed me that with hard work, dedication and commitment, anything is possible. Without them I would not be where I am today. They have been the backbone of everything.

My twin sister, Shannon, is my best friend and my best competitor. We spur each other on daily to be the best we can be. We always want the best for each other, no matter what. Also behind the glamour of the medals and personal bests, there's the gruelling training sessions, the relentless setbacks, the injuries and so much more. Shannon has seen me through everything – the good times and the bad, and vice versa.

Chrissy Ohuruogu is also an inspiration because she's such a fighter. The 2013 World Champs in Moscow made me think she's the GOAT (greatest of all time). To win that race by 0.004 seconds was phenomenal; her last 100m was simply brilliant! That was also the year when I transitioned from 300m to 400m, so watching that race gave me a real fire in my belly to attack the 400m and be brave.

Memories

Also in 2013, I ran the qualifying times for the World Youth Championships, but didn't perform at my best at the National Trials so I wasn't selected. I vowed to myself that I never again wanted to feel the way I did when I didn't get that selection phone call. Going into the 2014 season, my coach and I decided that we were going to step up our training, and in that year, I became the U20 400m national champion with a championship best performance.

At the 2018 Indoor National Champs, I fell flat on my face at the start of my 400m race. At the time, I was distraught because it was a chance for me to get my first Senior GBR vest. But now I look back at it and just die with laughter. I still have no idea how or why it happened.

ACHIEVEMENTS
European Junior Championships silver medal, 400m (2015)

European Junior Championships gold medal, 4 x 400m (2015)

SHANNON HYLTON

How I first became involved in sport

My mum got me into dancing when I was two years old. I was always jumping up and down as a kid, and she wanted to give me and my twin sister Cheriece something whereby we could blow off some steam. I secretly think she loved the idea of us being centre stage and in a tutu. I loved dancing and was still doing it 10 years later!

As for athletics, I was spotted in primary school. I remember a lady, Nanette Cross, coming into our school when I was in Year 5. She had organised running races for the class and I remember beating the fastest boys in the school. From then onwards, I began taking up athletics at the weekends for fun whilst still dancing five days a week. It has been a whirlwind of a journey since that day.

Inspiration

I have several sources of inspiration from different aspects of my life and each has its own reason. My family are my biggest supporters, and they have been with me every step of the way – my mum, dad and granny especially. From my father taking the laborious trips to different corners of the country for national championships, to my mother offering massages after competitions, their support has been profound. I remember in 2014, Cheriece and I had our first national competition together, the IAAF 2014 World Junior Championships in Eugene, Oregon. I was not expecting any family support out there because the trip there alone is very expensive. That was until I received a phone call from my granny saying that she'd landed at Eugene Airport and was asking me for directions to Hayward Field. I remember Cheriece was running in the 4 x 400m relay and my granny ensured she didn't miss it. She turned up two hours before the race was due to begin and was cheering all the way. If you watch the race back on YouTube, you can hear her cheers for Cheriece. That is a day I will never forget.

Another inspiration (albeit not athletic success) is my transition and growth as a person from 2016 to 2017 where I experienced my first major injuries, ruling me out of the 2016 Summer Olympic Games in Rio. I learned about my body, and how to deal with the unexpected in more ways than one. The setbacks were huge learning curves that I used as platforms for my return from injury in 2017.

Watching the London Olympics in 2012 really did inspire the 'next generation'. I remember seeing Jessica Ennis-Hill and Katarina Johnson-Thompson line up in the same 200m heptathlon race. Watching a race where two athletes representing Great Britain & Northern Ireland – one in the prime of her career and one at the start of her career – was a sight to see. Watching KJ-T achieve

ACHIEVEMENTS

European Junior Championships silver medal, 200m (Eskilstuna 2015)

European Junior Championships gold medal, 4 x 100m (Eskilstuna 2015)

British Outdoor Champion, 200m (2017)

so much at such a young age had me at home thinking, 'I would love to be on that track right now. A home Olympic Games ... could any moment be better than that?'

My final inspirations are two women quite close to home, who operate in South East London and other parts of the United Kingdom – Michelle Moore and Francesca Brown. I feel they have set a platform for me to become not only a better athlete, but a better person too. I attended a BE Unplugged event hosted by my university one evening and met these incredible women. They have started two initiatives, Moore Development and Goals4Girls respectively, which have given girls a belief and a window of opportunity that may not have existed if these organisations were not in place. They are established for girls to achieve their academic and sporting goals and abilities. As a sportswoman and student, I believe it is my responsibility to encourage the next generation of athletes. I am just refreshed and delighted to see two women already doing so, right on my doorstep.

$\Rightarrow$

Memories

Prior to the 2015 European Juniors, I had competed at the 2013 IAAF World Youth Championships and 2014 IAAF World Junior Championships and came 6th and 4th respectively. When I was at the European Juniors I finally received a medal, albeit silver rather than gold. From the post-race buzz and sorting out my hair and make-up for the medal ceremony, to taking my first step onto the podium and feeling the medal hung around my neck for the first time, I felt an incredible sense of pride representing my country. I remember I looked up to the crowd, took a deep breath in and thought, 'Wow, so this is what it feels like to win something! And it wasn't even gold.' I hold on to that feeling, it's my driver to becoming a better athlete.

The day I ran my first 400m race, I only made it to 390m. I left my blocks and set off like a train; 250m into the race I knew I was either going to die on the finish line or over it, and I didn't intend to die before it. I kept going, my focus on the finish line, but as I got to the final stretch, I tripped and fell flat on my face at 390m. It was the most embarrassing race experience of my life.

What I am doing now

Still training hard and aiming to become
an Olympic Champion.

The winning British team in the 4 x 100m relay, London 2018
Asha Philip, Shannon Hylton, Bianca Williams & Imani-Lara Lansiquot

ATHLETICS

DOROTHY HYMAN MBE

How I first became involved in sport

I competed at sport against other local schools in my native South Yorkshire, found I was quite good at running and enjoyed the thrill of winning. My father came to watch me run in an inter-school sports day and, although I didn't win that particular day, he could see that I had some talent and started taking me to my local park to train. Through a workmate, I was then introduced to a local coach who worked with a small group of sprinters. I joined my local athletics club and progressed from there right up to international competition.

Inspiration

My first inspiration was Heather Armitage, who was another local girl and international sprinter. I recall hearing about her doing well at the Melbourne Olympics in 1956, and the thrill I felt at competing in the same team as her and being encouraged by her. Oh yes, and beating her in later years – just before she retired!

Memories

I owe so much to my athletics and there were many outstanding moments. The sport gave me the opportunity to travel the world, open my horizons and meet a lot of very interesting people. It made me the person I am now.

ACHIEVEMENTS

Olympic Games silver medal, 100m (Rome 1960)
Olympic Games bronze medal, 200m (Rome 1960)
European Championships gold medal, 100m
(Belgrade 1962)
European Championships silver medal, 200m
(Belgrade 1962)
Commonwealth Games gold medal, 100yds (Perth 1962)
Commonwealth Games gold medal, 220yds (Perth 1962)

Appointed MBE in 1965
BBC Sports Personality of the Year, 1963

BOWLS

MARGARET JOHNSTON MBE

How I first became involved in sport

I was always interested in sport at school and played hockey and netball. However, I didn't start bowling until I was 20. I began by playing short mat bowls indoors, but one of the halls in which this took place was extensively damaged during the Troubles in Northern Ireland, when the pub opposite was blown up.

Inspiration

My ex-husband was invited to join an outdoor club in Ballymoney, NI, but I could only go inside the club three times a year because I wasn't a member. When I got fed up with freezing in the car outside, I decided to join. Eventually I entered the Irish Singles and reached the final in 1978 and the semi-final the following year. In 1981, I was selected for an international trial and made the team. I was to enjoy success for another 27 years.

Memories

When I was on the International Indoor team, there was a training weekend for which, curiously, one of the 'fitness' requirements was lying on a towel on a cold hard floor. Some of the team complained about having sore backs as a result, and received no sympathy from me. I thought it was ludicrous, and told them they shouldn't

ACHIEVEMENTS

World Outdoor Championships gold medal (Scotland 1992; Australia 2000 & England 2004)

Commonwealth Games gold medal (Canada 1994) World Indoor Championships gold medal (Wales 1988)

World Outdoor Championships gold medal, pairs (NZ 1988; Scotland 1992 & England 1996)

Commonwealth Games gold medal, pairs (Scotland 1986)

Appointed MBE in 1991
Woman Bowler of the Year on nine occasions
BBC Northern Ireland Sports Personality of the Year, 2004

do anything they weren't happy about!

I decided to take a break from indoor international competition. When I was asked why, I told the official that I had no problem with the bowling but the rest – including cold, hard floors – was a waste of time. I was told I had to and I replied I didn't, and my name was taken off the list. This inevitably attracted the attention of a sports reporter, who rang to ask why I was no longer on the team. Without thinking, I told him: 'If I was lying on my back on the floor I would like to think that I was at least enjoying myself.'

He kindly asked if he could print that and, of course, I said no when I realized what it implied. However, I relented when he offered me a brandy – and the bowling world thought it was a hoot. Apparently it made the Top 10 quotes of the year.

SHELLEY JORY-LEIGH

POWERBOAT RACING

How I first became involved in sport

The first sport I ever loved was horse riding, at the age of six in 1976. I was fearless, and the faster I could go and the higher I could jump was what I wanted at a young age. Being sent off to boarding school in 1978 opened up a whole host of sports for me – my favourite being gymnastics. But I also loved trampolining, high board diving, hockey, netball and swimming. I was basically a jack-of-all-trades, master of none yet loving every minute of it, and was often the team captain. One sport in which I did seem to do well, though not my favourite, was fencing – becoming national champion at 14. Fencing also helped me to get into the great sports school, Millfield for my A levels in 1987. So I was always very determined in the sports department and competitive at a young age. In the last six months I have returned to horse riding and have a great passion for skiing at great speed, along with my amazing powerboat racing career. ⇒

Inspiration

As I child, I would have huge posters on my wall of the Olympic gymnasts Nellie Kim and Nadia Comaneci, and be in absolute awe of them, never really thinking I would one day be a champion myself. To be honest, there was not a woman to look up to in the world of powerboat racing, but there were many men who I wanted to beat. I have this attitude: if *he* can do it so can I!

In the early 1990s, I would go with friends to watch the powerboat races in Cowes and Bournemouth, thinking it was a millionaires' club. However, we soon realized we could actually enter at a low level in the production class, which we did. It was a hobby at weekends, nothing more. Soon other racers realized that I was a good team player, organised, tough and well prepared, and was asked by other owners to join their teams and race with them. I guess my inspiration came from these men who put their trust in me to race alongside them. I was not going to let them down but do the very best job I could. I also like to win, and though in powerboat racing you are only competing for the power and the glory – no prize money – I liked the glory of standing on the podium alongside male competitors.

Memories

I have had to contend with both discouraging and encouraging moments in my sporting career. The discouragement came from some race organisers and the Officer of the Day. I was asked to produce an all-girl team, basically to meet the demands of political correctness and to look good. No one ever thought we would actually win! Even the prizes were men's watches with nothing for the ladies. Some seemed to think, if you are a woman winning in a man's world, you must be cheating. Regrettably, this was the attitude I often had to contend with during many years of powerboat racing. However, I kept persevering through all the scrutiny, rumours and protests, and it made me a stronger and better competitor. The prize was eventually gaining the respect of my male counterparts, which I have to this day. Gaining that respect was better than winning a race!

A major setback was most definitely a near-fatal racing accident in 2010. I was racing for a team called Spirit of Belgium in a brand new powerboat that had been specifically built to race offshore in the rough seas of Europe. Unfortunately, it had a complete structural failure and while racing in Sardinia at 90 mph, the boat came to a very abrupt halt. It's like driving a car into a brick wall at 90 mph without a seatbelt. In an ⇒

open powerboat you are not harnessed because, if it turns over, you need to be thrown clear. My full-faced crash helmet was a mess and had planted into my face. My co-driver was totally unconscious. It was a mess. I suffered eight months of concussion and had to have my nose re-built. The following year I decided to get back into a boat and try again, but this was a mistake as I was not ready. I made it to the end of the season through sheer stupidity and determination, but I really didn't enjoy it. I was devastated and thought I had lost my mojo forever. I spent the next four years repairing myself mentally and physically, not racing a full season but doing the odd invitation drive in the USA away from the limelight and pressure.

My fondest memory came in 2016 when a racing associate, who I didn't know that well, asked me if I would ever consider driving for him in the Cowes Torquay Cowes, the toughest offshore powerboat race in the world. He knew my history and the fact that I was nervous behind the wheel. I asked my husband Trevor – an experienced race engineer – to check the history of my friend's career and the boat's structure and all was good. It was a huge success. An amazing friendship was cemented and he got me back behind the wheel and actually enjoying racing again. Second place overall in the Cowes Torquay Cowes topped my ego – making me the most successful woman driver ever in this historic race.

I must admit that on a long endurance race of three or four hours, I often pee in my overalls! Trust me, there is no stopping in a powerboat race and, when you are being bounced around like a rag doll, a full bladder does not help your concentration. To be honest, by the time you finish a race your fireproof overalls are drenched in sweat and sea water anyway … so who would know?

In 2004, my first year in the British Honda Championships with my all-girl team, I was leading the fleet with just two laps of the race to go. Then the local dolphins came out to play with us. They loved it, we loved it, but Greenpeace did not. They stopped the race immediately and I saw my first-ever win taken away from me, as the officials decided to declare the race null and void. I was really furious and the onboard camera and speakers in our crash helmets picked up some delightful, blasphemous language as I gave vent to my feelings. It did not survive the TV edit, but it did make it to TV bloopers. Another TV rant, which was used several times on various programmes, involved Julia Bradbury interviewing me after a dreadful competition error. Racing on the Mersey in Liverpool, just outside Albert Docks, we got an amazing start and I was leading the 20-boat fleet. However, red mist set in and I completely missed the first turn. My navigator was calling it correctly but I completely ignored her. As this was completely out of character for my near-perfect team, 90% of the fleet followed me heading to the Isle of Man. Julia asked me at the end of the race what

ACHIEVEMENTS

British Honda Powerboat Championships winner (2005). My (only) all-girl team of two beat 40 men. We then finished on the podium for the next three seasons

World Championships (2008). First women competitors in the Powerboat P1 Evolution Class

Invited to join the Younger Brethren of Trinity House (2013) where I still feel out of my league surrounded by Lords, Admirals, Dames & Captains of Cunard

Cowes Torquay Cowes Powerboat Race 2nd (2016). Highest-placed woman driver in the history of the race. In that particular year, 14 boats left Cowes & only two finished in very rough bad conditions

had happened? I replied: 'Sh*t happens. Oh sh*t, I can't say that can I? Oh sh*t, I just did.' Julia Bradbury just stared at me, then fell about laughing. Soccer AM also picked up this incident, and the next morning the highlight of the program was: 'This is what happens when you put two girls in charge of a powerboat.' They then showed the clip of us leading the fleet and missing the mark, and dubbed our voices over the top talking about shoes, suggesting that was why we went wrong. It's difficult to explain, but it was funny on film.

What I am doing now

Since the accident I have enjoyed being on the other side of the camera and I have commentated and presented for TV on many races around the world. I also enjoy live commentating at the races as a presenter with Sir Robin Knox Johnston on our own programme for BBC Radio.

I now manage two powerboat teams, one new one and one experienced one. I officially retired from racing in 2017 but enjoy my role as an ambassador for the sport and encouraging new blood. I love to walk round the pits, and am delighted when many of the racers, male and female, come up to me and ask my opinion or help with something.

Horse riding has recently come back into my life, 44 years after it all started. I reach a half-century of my own this year, and I intend to do as much in the second half as I did in the first. My motto is: work hard, play hard!

Alongside my racing career, I also have successfully run a family Bridal Wear business with 12 staff from 1991 to the present day.

SHANNON KAVANAGH

How I first became involved in sport

I came from a sporting family. My father wanted to be good but never was (those are his own words). His sister is a different story – she's my aunt, Mary Peters. I got involved as I loved being active. I was competitive, enjoyed competition and pushing myself to my best ability. My family was also interested in sport and I followed my sister into it. Walking out of school one day, when I was 10, a man was handing out leaflets to have tennis lessons. I went home and begged my parents to let me try. They did and the rest is history.

Inspiration

Reading about my Aunt Mary's achievements really inspired me. She had achieved some amazing personal performances through hard work and dedication. Having a relative like Mary is an inspiration in itself. She was always positive about everything I wanted to do in sport. As I get older my children and sport itself inspire me to keep competing to the best of my ability.

A great many people playing professional sport don't make any money; like me they just about break even. After growing up in Australia, I played two years of club tennis in Germany (they pay you to play for them and that covered my time in Europe). When at home I would deliver the local paper to earn money, painted friends' houses, did household chores and played local tournaments so I could afford my next trip. I travelled to many remote places and am glad I had the opportunity to play tennis.

When I retired from the tennis circuit in 1996 I was very keen to keep fit and wanting still to be competitive I started playing soccer, which was a nice change going from an individual sport to a team

> "My father wanted to be good but never was (those are his own words). His sister is a different story – she's my aunt, Mary Peters."

sport. I have continued to play football on and off for the last 10–15 years. I had time off to have my four beautiful children (but played in between having them) and to train for and compete in those 2009 World Masters Games. I also ran a Marathon in 2012.

Memories

When I was in Northern Ireland Mary bought me a brown Triumph in which to get around. I called it 'The Brown Bomber'. Whilst travelling home one night I was stopped by an army security patrol and asked for my driving licence (which I had actually acquired in Tennessee). The guy checking it called all his mates over to check out my licence and they reckoned it was from a supermarket in the States.

When I first arrived in America all the Americans wanted me to do was talk, as they thought my Aussie accent was hilarious. I pointed out that theirs was just as funny. They also thought we had kangaroos as pets, no electricity or running water. I use to say that we rode kangaroos to school and they believed it.

While travelling on the tennis circuit I did things like sleeping in airports overnight. One year I backpacked the circuit, stayed in youth hostels and was always able to do some sightseeing. The best sightseeing was when I played in Munich. I got to explore the city where Mary won her gold medal, and that was breathtaking.

While playing club tennis in Germany I got to experience the great thrill of being a passenger in a BMW doing 220km/hr on the autobahn. That's something you don't do everyday.

ACHIEVEMENTS

World Master Games silver medal (Age 40–44), pentathlon (Sydney 2009)

State representative tennis & soccer (last year of high school). Winners of national titles in both

Selected for Australia Girls International team, soccer (but chose to go to the US on a tennis scholarship)

Tennis Scholarship, Austin Peay State University (Clarksville, Tennessee)

Inducted into the University's Sporting Hall of Fame

World-ranked Pro Tennis Player (highest 292 in singles & 185 in Doubles)

Won first $10,000 tournament in Mildura, Australia

What I am doing now

I'll never forget Aunty Mary telling me (after she beat me in a race on her track, when I was eight), 'the faster you pump your arms, the faster your legs will follow'. Her coach Buster McShane had told her that. I am now an athletics coach and still say it to all my athletes and, of course, my own children. 🔥

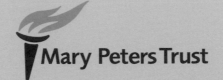

Mary Peters Trust

The Mary Peters Trust is Northern Ireland's premier sporting charity.

The Mary Peters Trust was established in 1975 to create an ongoing and meaningful commemoration of Lady Mary's Gold Medal victory in the 1972 Olympic Games in Munich. The Trust supports talented young sportsmen and women, both able-bodied and disabled, from across Northern Ireland to help them achieve their sporting dreams and ambitions. The Trust does this by selecting athletes across all sporting disciplines, financially supporting them and providing access to a team of experts to assist them on their pathway to success. This proven formula has delivered Olympic, Paralympic, World, European, Commonwealth, British and Irish Champions.

MAEVE KYLE OBE

ATHLETICS & HOCKEY

How I first became involved in sport

As a child, I lived in a boys' school where my father was headmaster. Sport was our leisure activity. We were very active children who revelled in playing all sports at whatever level we could. I liked to win but largely played sport to enjoy it and have fun. I remember that learning the skills and rules of the many sports we enjoyed was important – we were competitive but fair! Sport was our social activity, and an invitation to 'go out and play' meant joining in any sport available, always with a ball of some shape and size. We also learned to swim, cycle, climb and run (paper chases were very popular) as part of daily life.

Inspiration

My parents believed sport was essential for physical, mental and emotional development and they were both supportive and inspirational. They were very down-to-earth about winning and losing and working hard to be better, especially where skills were concerned. They were hugely supportive when we were competing at any level and, crucially, we always received an honest assessment of our performance.

Memories

The best thing about sport is the friends you make, and keep. We all go through highs and lows, laughter and tears, success and failure, and learn many life-useful lessons on the journey. Sport is probably one of the most influential factors in our lives and can be active or passive – taking part or coaching, being very competitive or just playing for fun, or for health and social activity.

Sports people experience every emotion, many disciplines and rules, and the greatest gifts of friendship and respect at every level.

ACHIEVEMENTS

European Indoor Championships bronze medal, 400m (Dortmund 1966)

Olympic Games competitor 400m (Melbourne 1956 & Rome 1960)

Olympic Games semi-finals, 400m & 800m (Tokyo 1964)

58 hockey caps for Ireland over 20 years

Represented Leinster, Munster & Ulster at different stages of her career

Appointed OBE in 2008

Installed into Irish Hockey Hall of Fame, 2006

Member of World All Star team, 1953 & 1959

AVRIL LENNOX MBE

ACHIEVEMENTS

All England Gymnastics Champion:
1973, 1974, 1975

British Gymnastics Champion:
1974, 1975, 1976 & 1977

British Apparatus Champion
(four disciplines): 1972–1977

Olympic Games competitor (Munich
1972) & finalist (Montreal 1976)

Appointed MBE in 1977

First British gymnast to be awarded the
Winston Churchill Memorial Travelling
Scholarship (1973), presented by
Prince Charles

Inspiration

The magic of the Olympics is something that captivated me as a child. So my aim in Munich (1972), as the youngest member of the British gymnastics team, was to gain valuable experience for the future. This was fully realized when I not only competed against, but also witnessed the extraordinary performances of the tiny Russian gymnast, Olga Korbut. Although her team-mate, Ludmilla Tourischeva, won the individual gold medal, it was Olga who captured the hearts of millions around the world for her dazzling acrobatic skills.

My second Olympics in 1976 in Montreal, Canada was a greater achievement. Having moved to London from Leicester to increase my training hours and to access National coaching, I travelled to the Montreal Olympics well prepared.

Rubbing shoulders with gymnastic icons such as Nadia Comaneci from Romania and Olga Korbut was an amazing experience and a real inspiration and motivator for me to succeed. Having competed on all four pieces of apparatus over two days, I became the first British Gymnast to reach the All-Around finals of the Olympic Games.

I feel extremely privileged to have competed in an era alongside these stars who, together with Tourischeva and Nellie Kim, were credited with popularising the sport around the world.

Memories

During the Montreal Olympics, when I became the first British Gymnast to qualify for the All-Around finals, my improved performance was met with surprise from the Olympic competition organisers ... so much so, I was drug tested twice. Although both times I passed with flying colours, this experience left me feeling extremely low. Mary Peters, who was commentating during the Games, noticed the impact the drug-testing had on me, so offered to cheer me up. She took me to downtown Montreal to a radio studio. I wasn't really in the mood for a radio interview, but reluctantly went along with the idea. Little did I know that, once in the studio, Mary set up a live radio link with Terry Wogan in London and my parents at home in Oadby, Leicester. It was so reassuring

to talk to my mum and dad and to chat with Terry. Mary was right of course, the experience really did cheer me up. I'll always be grateful to her for that.

I cannot ignore the fact that I will remember my first Olympic experience for something other than sport. In the early hours of 5th September, 1972 eight Palestinian terrorists broke into the Olympic Village, killed two members of the Israeli team and took nine more hostage. Like many Olympians I witnessed the terrorist activities unfold from my apartment overlooking the tragedy. After hours of tense negotiations, the terrorists and hostages were flown to a military airport in Munich. A horrifying gun battle ensued claiming the lives of all nine hostages. I found it extremely difficult to fully comprehend the events of that day, but when I attended the memorial service in the Olympic stadium and saw the Olympic flag flying at half-mast, the realisation hit me and I felt emotionally empty.

What I am doing now

Sport has remained a major part of my life. When I retired from competitive gymnastics I took up golf and represented the Leicestershire County Women's team. I also set up my own gymnastics club and coached gymnasts to international standard. Now, as a Leisure Development Manager, my experiences throughout my working life have inspired me to encourage people of all ages to take up sport and lead a more active life. 🔥

GABBY LOGAN
GYMNASTICS & PRESENTING

How I first became involved in sport

Sport was forever in my blood. My dad (Terry Yorath) was a professional footballer and so we grew up in a very sporty household. I loved all sport, but from a young age wanted to be a tennis player. I played netball, ran and did all the activities at school. But gymnastics was the one I really fell for and, at the age of 10, I joined a new club in Leeds and my gymnastics life took off.

Inspiration

I had an amazing coach in Leeds, Anne Tallintyre, who was also one of the National Squad coaches. I progressed quickly and, within a few years, I was training with that squad myself. A clutch of Russian and Bulgarian gymnasts dominated the sport when I first started. They were 'otherworldly' creatures, capable of incredible beauty and great athleticism. I watched old tapes of their routines for hours on end and tried hard to emulate them. Every spare minute I had was spent making up moves and routines and listening to potential music

ACHIEVEMENTS

British Rhythmic Gymnastics Championships silver medal, 1990

Commonwealth Games, coming 8th (Auckland 1990)

National Squad Member, British Rhythmic Gymnastics (1986–1990)

to accompany them. If I wasn't training, I was designing leotards or doing extra ballet at home. I was also inspired by two British gymnasts, Jacquie Leavy and Lorraine Priest, who went to the Olympic Games in Los Angeles in 1984.

Memories

I was once competing in a three-way rhythmic gymnastics international in Wakefield, against Australia and New Zealand ahead of the Commonwealth Games. I managed to throw my ribbon up and get it stuck in the ceiling. They had to bring on a crane and stop the competition in order to get it down. It was petulance on my part as I had kept doing it during warm-up, so I knew the ceiling was low. I should have altered my throw. You live and learn.

What I am doing now

I am one of the BBC's prime time TV sport presenters, covering a number of top-level events including football, rugby union and athletics. I am also one of the co-presenters of the annual BBC Sports Personality of the Year Award programme.

CURLING

RHONA MARTIN MBE (NÉE HOWIE)

How I first became involved in sport

I played hockey, badminton and swimming at school, but when I was leaving I wanted to try something different so I took up curling. My brother played and had just won the Scottish Championships and it looked like fun. I took it up as a social sport but after a very short time I became extremely competitive and successful!

Inspiration

Steve Redgrave, the five-time Olympic gold medal-winning rower. I watched a documentary about him several times – about his mindset and team leadership qualities. It really inspired me to lead a team of my own, and taught me so much about coping with setbacks and defeat, and how to bounce back even stronger.

Memories

My Olympic gold medal was stolen from a museum in Dumfries three years ago and I have been unable to get a replica made. There has been no sign of the original one, and this saddens me as I loved inspiring schoolchildren with it.

Before the Salt Lake City Olympics in 2002 we were practising at a GB training Centre in Austria, which had a lot of snow. We were training on a small rink that was extremely cold, so while I was on the ice, I put my outdoor boots on the radiator pipes so they would be cosy. When I came off the ice the soles of my boots had melted all round the pipe!

What I am doing now

I am currently the High Performance Manager for Bowls, Scotland

ACHIEVEMENTS

Olympic Games gold medal (GB team), curling (Salt Lake City 2002)
Olympic Games GB team (Turin 2006)
European Championships (team) silver medal (1998)
World Championships competitor (2000)
Six European Championships between 1996–2006
Scottish Women's Championship team winners (2000)
Coach to GB team, bronze medal winners (Sochi 2014)

Appointed MBE in 2002

HOCKEY & GOLF

VIOLET McBRIDE

ACHIEVEMENTS

Olympic Games GB squad
(hockey), vice-captain
(Seoul 1988)

Ireland International, hockey
(including two World Cups)

Ulster U21 hockey

Ulster Schoolgirls hockey, Captain

Ireland Senior Ladies
representative (golf) including
Home Internationals & European
Team Championships

Inducted into the Irish Hockey
Association Hall of Fame, 2011

**With Carl Lewis at the opening
of the Seoul 1988 Olympics**

How I first became involved in sport

I was introduced to hockey as a schoolgirl at Kilkeel High School in Northern Ireland,
and was inspired by my PE teacher, Valerie Cromwell. I then played at Portadown HC
and the Ulster College of Physical Education. Golf was an extra-curricular activity at
school, but I attended regularly.

Inspiration

My uncle encouraged me by taking me out to play at Kilkeel Golf Club. He insisted that
I play off the men's tees, which might have seemed a little unfair at the time but was
helpful in the long run.

Memories

While at the Olympics in Seoul I received a shamrock pin from Mary Peters prior to
the start of the tournament. Also prior to the Olympics in Japan, I played volleyball with
Daley Thompson who was my sporting hero (next to Mary, of course).

HOCKEY

SHIRLEY McCAY

How I first became involved in sport

I always loved to play football when I was at primary school, and am an avid fan of Liverpool FC. I got involved in hockey in secondary school largely due to the positive influences of my former PE teacher, Mary Swan.

Inspiration

Growing up as a Liverpool fan, footballer Steven Gerrard was my big inspiration. I loved his work rate, energy and passion to drive his team forward. I thought he was always humble, never seeking the spotlight and quietly getting on with his work, wanting to be better every day. Mary Peters is of course an inspiration to me as well. I remember my mum talking about her when I was young. As a local heroine, she continues to inspire both old and new generations of young sports people aspiring to do great things. She is simply a remarkable woman and a role model for so many.

Memories

The 2018 tournament with Ireland was so special, in that we achieved something we never thought possible by reaching a World Cup final – the first for any team sport in Ireland. Going way back, my first cap, against Canada in South Africa in 2007, was also an incredible feeling!

On the flip side of that I have had some really painful moments. In 2016 we missed out on Rio Olympic Qualification on penalties, by the width of a post. However, our failings only spurred us on to be better, and two years on we were World Cup silver medallists!

On more than one occasion, when I have come off as a substitute, I have sat down accidentally on the wrong team's bench. When you're playing in tough conditions and are a bit out of breath, often you forget! It's a rather embarrassing moment when you have to get up gingerly and go to the right bench.

What I am doing now

At the moment I work full time as a Talent Coach for Ulster Hockey, overseeing our underage performance programmes and hopefully producing the next top hockey talent. I am still a member of the Irish Hockey team.

ACHIEVEMENTS

World Cup silver medal for Ireland (London 2018)

Played in six European Championships & three Olympic Qualifiers

Most-capped female athlete in any Irish Sport (273 caps)

Ambassador for the Mary Peters Trust

LIZ McCOLGAN MBE

How I first became involved in sport

My PE teacher at school was a marathon runner so during PE class he would send us out on runs around the school. He enrolled me in athletics at school and at the local club.

Inspiration

There were two people in particular. One was Steve Ovett, who I saw as working class with a great work ethic. When I met him as an 18 year-old he was really encouraging. He knew all about me, what races I was doing and really motivated me to run well. The other was the Norwegian athlete Grete Waitz. She led the way in women's distance running, especially the marathon. She was such an inspiration and wonderful person and I was honoured when she became my coach later in my career.

Memories

A friend once said to me: 'I don't know what all the fuss is about in these races. Why don't you just get to the front and stay there?' I recall telling her, 'I wish it was that easy.'

What I am doing now

I coach my daughter Eilish, who is presently one of GB's best 5,000m and 10,000m runners, and who has been to the Olympics and World Championships. I now reside in Doha, Qatar, where I have set up my own athletic training club for all abilities. It's a challenge, but I have discovered some great runners out here.

Fellow celebrities Nell McAndrew, Ben Fogle and Gavin Hastings with Liz at Castle Urquhart before the first Monster Duathalon

ACHIEVEMENTS

World Championships gold medal, 10,000m (Tokyo 1991)

Olympic Games silver medal, 10,000m (Seoul 1988)

Commonwealth Games gold medals, 10,000m (Edinburgh 1986 & Auckland 1990)

Commonwealth Games bronze medal, 3,000m (Auckland 1990)

World Indoor Championships silver medal, 3,000m (Budapest 1989)

World Cross-country Championship silver medal (Warsaw 1987) & bronze medal (Amoriebieta 1991)

Winner London (1996), New York (1991) & Tokyo (1992) marathons

World Half Marathon champion (Newcastle 1992)

Appointed MBE in 1992

BBC Sports Personality of the Year, 1991

Inducted into the Scottish Sports Hall of Fame, 2004

DIANNE McMILLAN MBE (NÉE BARR)

PARALYMPIC SWIMMING

How I first became involved in sport

I was involved in swimming from a very young age, encouraged greatly by my parents. I enjoyed training and competing and not only did it keep me fit and healthy, but allowed me to build great friendships and to travel. I initially competed at club level with Larne Swimming Club and then at national level in England (Sport for the Disabled). My first introduction to international competition was at the age of 14 in 1987.

> "My first introduction to international competition was at the age of 14 ..."

Inspiration

When I started swimming I was very young, so I wasn't particularly inspired by anyone. I did it because I loved it. I looked up to the older club members and aspired to be like them. In later years, I followed the achievements of Duncan Goodhew and Sarah Hardcastle, and was impressed by their success.

Memories

I remember learning to dive, which was quite tricky and sometimes daunting on one leg. In order to develop this skill, my coaches encouraged me to balance my stump on a chair. This seemed to work well and I continued to use it for a period of time. However, on one occasion when I was competing in a club event, I dived in and the chair fell into the water behind me. I ignored it and continued swimming while they fished it out. Thankfully, I mastered diving from the blocks very soon afterwards.

ACHIEVEMENTS

Paralympic double gold medallist (Seoul 1988)

Paralympic silver & bronze medallist (Seoul 1988)

Paralympic bronze medal, 100m backstroke (Barcelona 1992)

World Championship gold & silver medallist (The Netherlands 1987)

European Championship triple gold medallist (Paris 1987)

Appointed MBE in 2016

ROWING

LIZ McVEIGH (NÉE PATON)

How I first became involved in sport

I was an avid television observer, with my parents, of international athletics and many other sports from a young age. But I was the one at school who could not easily co-ordinate eye with bat or ball (lacrosse in the winter and rounders/tennis in the summer) and therefore considered myself 'non-sporty'. I went to university where I found exercise largely through walking up and down the hills of Bristol to and from lectures, the pub and friends' houses … .

I applied for jobs post-university and a 'gap year' and found that the interesting jobs were in London. Horror! I didn't wish to spend my life in what I saw as the 'Big Smoke'! But two days after my 23rd birthday in November 1975, I took up a position with the Civil Service's Centre for Overseas Pest Research in Kensington and found a place in a flat in Chiswick.

After a couple of weeks, I could bear it no longer and took a cycle ride to find the green spaces of West London to help me cope with city life. I found the Civil Service Sports Ground where a number of bat and ball activities were offered. I explained my anxiety over this and was directed over the mound towards the river and the Civil Service Boathouse.

Upon knocking tentatively at the door, it was opened by one of the members and I explained that I was looking for a sport and a way to enjoy life in London. I had barely opened my mouth when they welcomed me with open arms, and even more encouragingly, a pint of lager. For once my size (close to 6ft) was a good thing.

Inspiration

Once I had explained about the rowing thing to my parents, many anecdotes came out of the closet. It turned out my father had rowed whilst studying on an agricultural course for a year in Reading, just after marrying my mother in 1934. My mother also took the challenge and entered a competition at Laleham Regatta that same year. We still have the silver cup she won in her one and only race.

Then a pair of blue eyes at work caught my attention, especially as they encouraged me to take up the sport that they had enjoyed so much. These blue eyes belonged to the man (husband Lawrence) whom I was to marry in 1980 after my return from the Moscow Olympics.

Then there was the inspiration of joining a club that contained members going to the first Olympic Games to hold Women's rowing events (Montreal, 1976), plus members who had only just missed selection. International aspirations became feasible, even for someone who had considered themselves 'non-sporty' for 23 years, once I found I could compete on level terms with these other members.

Memories

I recall my first exposure to the press, a half-page feature on the back of the *Sunday Times*, covering international trials in Nottingham in the autumn of 1977. This was my first time at trials. I was not very fit after a few weeks off with a cracked rib, and I did not help any of the crews I was in. So the photo on the back page was of a pair of rowers, wearing the most bizarre collection of woolly hats and tops to keep off the wind and rain, at the back of the pack and therefore nearest the camera in

the following launch. This was me and the long-suffering Chris Grimes.

In the spring of 1978 I had moved on and was more regularly at the other end of the pack, but still not confident about my abilities compared with others with a longer rowing and sporting pedigree. My friends still tease me about the time we were asked to list the top four athletes in a written note to the coaches. Apparently, I was the only one not to include myself in the crew.

The Olympic Games in Moscow was a wonderful experience, despite the political backdrop. In some ways the fact that we were not allowed to join the parade at the opening ceremony made it a better experience for us. We were able to enjoy the whole thing from the stands.

Another of the things that stuck in my mind was the plates of food eaten by those from different sports in the athletes' village. From huge piles of whatever took their fancy for the average rower, to delicate slices of tomato and lean ham for the gymnasts from the Eastern bloc. It would be interesting to compare eating habits at current Games, and what the competitors are offered or insist upon!

ACHIEVEMENTS

Olympic Games eight (Moscow 1980)
World Championships eight (Bled 1979)
European Regattas in a four & pair (1978)
GB National Rowing Squad (1977)
Medals from all bar one of the World Masters' Championships & many national events, 1997–2011 inclusive
Gap of 17 years before taking up competitive rowing again at Masters' level

ATHLETICS

KATHARINE MERRY

How I first became involved in sport

I took up gymnastics when I was very young and enjoyed it. However, a PE teacher – not at my school but one who lived two doors down from us – noticed my speed when I was playing in the road where I lived, and suggested to my parents that I should try athletics. My father was an English Schools triple jump medallist in the 1960s and still did a bit of running. I gave up the gymnastics when I was about 10 and started athletics. I was good and enjoyed it a lot.

Inspiration

It was the encouraging words of that teacher which made me think about running and gave me the belief that I could be quite good. My parents were supportive, of course, and my first club experience was an excellent one, which I think was vital to enjoying it and wanting to go back.

I started running seriously in the early 1980s so was inspired inevitably by watching the LA Olympic Games and seeing Daley Thompson, Seb Coe and, in particular, Kathy Cooke who won a bronze in the 400m. She was my big hero.

Memories

I remember standing in front of my parents and older brother when on holiday in 1984, watching the LA Olympics and saying to them that one day I would do what Kathy Cooke did ... win an Olympic medal. My brother laughed, of course, and I am not sure my parents were totally convinced, but hey, 16 years later, in Sydney it really happened for me! 🔥

ACHIEVEMENTS
Olympic Games bronze medal, 400m (Sydney 2000)
UK record holder, 200m indoors (22.83secs, 1999)

SHEILA MORROW

How I first became involved in sport

Both my mother and my father were keen sports people. Some of my earliest memories as a child are of going on alternate Saturdays, to watch my mother play hockey or my father play football, then going to the local church hall in the evening to play badminton with both of them and my brother. It was tennis as a family in the summer. When I went to Bangor Grammar School for Girls, it was only natural for me to play every sport that was going, for which I was hugely encouraged by my PE teacher, Mrs Renee Williams.

Inspiration

Initially, I wasn't particularly focused on hockey as I was a decent tennis player, competed in the hurdles and high jump for Caernarfonshire schools in the National Athletics Championships, and in badminton for the county too.

However, in 1964, I was selected to play hockey for the first ever North Wales Schoolgirls team against South Wales, which brought me to the attention of the senior Welsh selectors. That resulted in an invitation to attend a summer school at Lilleshall National Sports Centre where I received coaching for the first time and had the opportunity to play alongside members of the current Welsh team. What an eye opener and inspiration! Seeing their skill on the ball and the way that were able to read the game, made me determined to emulate them and awakened my desire to play for my country.

Memories

I almost didn't realize my dream as, in 1965, I went to college in Liverpool at I.M. Marsh College of Physical Education. I struggled to gain a place in the college first team and almost gave it up to play lacrosse.

In my second year at college, I was invited to the North Wales senior trials but had to turn the invitation down as the date clashed with college matches against another PE college. In those days there was no question that college events took precedence over any other commitment. However, on the day of the trials, it snowed and the college matches were cancelled so a friend and I hitchhiked to Wrexham where the trials were due to take place. I was lucky enough to be selected for the first team, played against South Wales, was invited to the Welsh trials, was selected for the Welsh team, and held my place for the next 16 years!

In 1980, women's hockey was included for the first time in the Olympic Games due to be held in Moscow and I was lucky enough to be selected to play for Great

Sheila (r) captaining Wales against England 1981

Britain in all the qualifying matches. I became so excited to think that I would actually get to compete at the Olympic Games. It was therefore a cruel blow when the hockey authorities decided to comply with a UK government request that sports should boycott the Games, especially as we were one of only three sports that did so.

I was still in the squad four years later but unfortunately we narrowly missed qualifying for the Los Angeles Games, so I never did get to play at an Olympics, although I was lucky enough to attend both the 2008 Beijing and 2012 London Games as an International Technical Official, which was the next best thing.

⇒

I think that my proudest moment came in 1981 when I captained Wales against England at Wembley and got to introduce the team to the Queen who was attending the annual match for the first time. To step out onto the hallowed turf in front of 65,000 schoolgirls and meet the Queen was an experience I will never forget. It's one for which I am eternally grateful to both my PE teacher and my parents who inspired, encouraged and supported me all my career.

What I am doing now

I am still involved in hockey as a Technical Official – my latest appointment being as Competition Director for the Women's Tournament at the Glasgow Commonwealth Games. I can honestly say that I owe the game so much in terms of the friends I have made, the places I have visited and the experiences I have had. To any young person who has a similar opportunity I would say 'grab it with both hands.' If you get only a small percentage of the pleasure I have had, your life will be much richer.

ACHIEVEMENTS

Olympic Games, GB Team, hockey (Moscow 1980). The team was withdrawn after a Government-requested boycott

Olympic Games, GB squad, qualifying (Los Angeles 1984)

Captain, Wales v England (Wembley 1981) & Welsh international squad member for 16 years

North Wales Junior Champion, tennis (1964)

ATHLETICS

TINA MUIR

How I first became involved in sport

I didn't like long-distance running at first, even hiding in the toilets at school when they were selecting people to run in a local competition. After running cross-country in PE lessons, I ended up on the school team, and found out that I actually liked it and was decent at it. I found a local coach, Brad Plummer, who was supportive, and helped me train, but was determined to make sure I was not pushed too hard at a young age. As Brad helped me move up the ranks, I really fell in love with running, and have felt the same ever since.

Inspiration

Paula Radcliffe. When I first started running, I did not really follow big events at all. I doubt I even knew how far a marathon was. One year I went to watch the London Marathon, and I remember Paula running past me on her way to a World record. That moment inspired me more than any other – she looked so strong, and I thought it was incredible. I followed her from then on, admiring her guts, and refusal to back down.

I don't think grit is something you can teach, and it is something I have always prided myself on. Seeing Paula running so well always inspired me to want to be the best I could be, and that some day my race would be the marathon. I always knew in my heart that my breakthrough would come, and without Paula as a role model, I would never have had that dream.

Memories

In a 10,000m race a few years ago, I went out too fast, and ended up hanging on from a long way out. In the final 400m, my body started shutting down. I fell twice running down the final straight, the second time just one metre before the end. I pretty much crawled across the finish line! To make it even worse, that race was being filmed, and the cameras were focused on me perfectly as I fell.

ACHIEVEMENTS

**Olympic Games GB trials,
10,000m (3rd, 2012)**

**Winner, Walt Disney World
Half Marathon (2019)**

ATHLETICS

HAYLEY MURRAY

ACHIEVEMENTS

Northern Ireland record holder, hammer

Northern Ireland hammer champion (2013 & 2014)

English Schools winner three times

Sixth in World Schools Championships (2006)

How I first became involved in sport

I became involved in athletics while I was in primary school. A friend invited me to cross-country sessions after school and from there I got signposted to a local athletics club. I gave pretty much everything a go until I eventually tried the hammer throw when I was 14. Immediately I loved the event and started to progress faster than in any other I had tried.

Inspiration

The year I started my hammer throwing was the year Dame Kelly Holmes won the two gold medals in the Athens Olympics. I remember watching her on TV and wanting to be like her. I craved her success, and remember pushing myself really hard in training sessions just to know that I'd given my all in the athletic season, like Kelly would have done.

Memories

I competed at the UK Schools International in Tullamore, Ireland in 2006. I have always competed where there are nets and cage doors, but when I got there, I noticed they had neither nets nor doors but chain link fencing instead. When I asked for the area with cage doors and netting, the Irish officials had no idea what we were on about and said 'We might end up getting them in another 20 years. This is Ireland for you.' It did make me smile.

CAMOGIE

AOIFE NI CHAISIDE

How I first became involved in sport

It was inevitable that I would play camogie as both parents were active club members and past players. My six siblings and were encouraged to attend trainings and matches for our club. From that it was a natural progression to play for our schools, county and university teams. I believe our Gaelic games have an important influence in our local community, encouraging young people to improve playing skills as well as life skills, developing as players and people.

Inspiration

My mammy and daddy granted us every opportunity in life, not only sport. They took us to matches to watch our local heroes play, and further afield to attend the biggest camogie events on the calendar – encouraging us to improve and practise our skills, and pushing us on a little if and when required. They shared their passion with us, which is now engraved in our hearts. My father trained a lot of hurling teams throughout the years but eventually he moved over to the camogie scene and my two sisters and I played under the management of himself and his good friend Dominic McKinley, right up to daddy's death in October 2016. More recently, my two sisters have also been my inspirations.

It is difficult to explain as I've grown up playing with them, but my mother always said when we were young: 'I can't wait to when my three girls are all playing on the one team'. The three of us played together in the Derry Senior Championship final, 2012, which we won, the first time in the club's history. However, it was special lining out alongside them in the all-Ireland in Croke Park in March, 2017 with mammy watching from the stand ... all of us thinking how proud daddy would have been to share in the occasion.

ACHIEVEMENTS

Winning the Senior All-Ireland Club Championship 2016/17 with Sleacht Néill must be the greatest in my mind. We also went on to win it the following two years, the first team in Ulster to achieve this. Playing for my county, Derry, in 2012 also stands out, as we won the All-Ireland Intermediate final, which went to a replay. At the age of 18 and playing full back, I thought it couldn't get much better than that. As far as individual awards, I attended the *Irish Times* Sports Women Awards event with my mother in Dublin where I was awarded March Sportswoman of the month. This was a lovely occasion spent among other great sports women of Ireland, but most importantly with my own hero by my side.

⟹

Memories

Following our first club county championship in 2012, we were well beaten in the following two years, emotions which I will not forget. Another painful memory was losing the All-Ireland Senior Schools reply final to Loreto, Kilkenny. We lost the game to a last-minute goal, a missed opportunity, and I left the pitch that day heartbroken. On the same pitch, many years later (2016) I would collect the Senior Ulster Championship as captain of the Sleacht Néill camogie team, a week-and-a-half after my father's death – a painful yet precious moment.

One of my most embarrassing moments while playing camogie was following an U16 or 18 'B' championship match for my club. We only had 13 or 14 players for a 15-a-side game, but our opponents decided to play 15 against us, which I was fuming about. We battled hard and the game was very tight but in the end we lost. When the whistle blew, I shook my marker's hand and said a few nasty things. When I went into the changing room afterwards, I thought of what I had said and was mortified at myself. I went home and told the story and when I told it out loud, I was even more cross with myself. In the heat of the moment, I was a sore loser and I had let myself down. I could do nothing but apologise to the player soon afterwards, someone I knew well from being on the same county team. But I learned from that experience, and have never allowed myself to act the same way since … I felt dreadful for letting myself and my family down.

What I am doing now

I think every sports person continues to strive for improvements. I'm trying to stay as fit as possible to play the highest level of camogie for my club and county for as long as possible. Off the pitch, I've recently presented a TV series on Women in Sport, looking at what has been achieved and the challenges we face. Analysing and supporting upcoming camogie matches is another thing I still like to do.

ATHLETICS
KERRY O'FLAHERTY

How I first became involved in sport

I was a very active child. My grandfather always took my brother and I out walking in Bangor; we collected conkers in the autumn and enjoyed walks to the beach in summer. Unless it was absolutely lashing down with rain we would always be outside playing with friends at home, which would involve running and chasing games. When I was 13, there was a 5,000m fun run at home in Newcastle (NI) and I asked my dad if I could run.

I beat most of the boys that day and that's when my home club Newcastle AC scooped me up.

Inspiration

Over the years my family have inspired me to keep on running and competing. My parents took me to many a muddy field in the early days to run and my grandfather, Fred, was always so proud of me. He was the first person I would call after a race. He encouraged me so much as a child – I would watch the athletics on TV with him. It's hard not having him around any more, but I know that a lot of my strength and determination comes from him.

Mary Peters has always been a great support to me, especially with her inspirational chats. She always knows just what to say, and is one of the most knowledgeable people that I know. Mary helped teach me how to be mentally strong, and I carry her autobiography with me on training camps and to big races. It's a fantastic read and is very inspiring. There really is 'something about Mary'.

Jo Pavey has been one of my role models for many years – especially since I met her at a British Milers Club meeting. She is in her 40s now and an amazing athlete. Her European gold medal performance in the 10,000m in Zurich in 2014, 10 months after having her second child, was remarkable. She certainly inspired me. If I can be as strong as Jo then why wouldn't I go for the Tokyo Olympics in 2020 and the 2022 Commonwealth Games in Birmingham?

Memories

I have made many trips to Font Romeu in the French Pyrenees for altitude training (6,000ft). The weather is usually fabulous, but in the mountains a cold snap can bring snow at almost any time. When we were there some years ago, Irish 800m runner Roseanne Gilligan and I woke one morning to find snow everywhere – 3ft on the ground, on the cars, falling off trees into drifts. Our first thoughts, like all athletes, were about our training. We were due to run a 'tempo session' which required us to run reasonably quickly for several miles, but impossible in the conditions that greeted us. Resilience is a big factor in any athlete's mentality so we dug the car out, took advantage of a snow plough and drove to Spain, 2,000ft lower, just to train. Sure enough it was cold but clear. We set off, but when we were near the end of the run the snow arrived there too. Undeterred we set off back up the mountain in the car to our apartment. Inevitably a new blanket of snow had fallen and our car got slower and slower until it just stopped. Soon we had a deep drift both in front of us and behind us, and we were in the middle of nowhere. There was an old uninhabited farmhouse nearby and we found a hoe with which we tried to extract ourselves. No chance! Eventually I called Northern Ireland on my mobile, and asked my coach Richard to phone the local French council and tell them of our predicament. Amazingly, it worked and another snow plough was sent to dig us out. The look of disbelief on the driver's face, when we told him we'd been 'running', was something I'll never forget. It turned out that GB 800m runner Jenny Meadows and other members of UK Athletics had ventured out and got stuck for a time too. We were so relieved to be rescued, we spent the rest of the day drinking hot chocolate and giggling about how silly we were. We thought it had all blown over until we appeared on the front of the local paper; a great souvenir for two crazy Irish runners who went to ridiculous lengths to get in their training.

ACHIEVEMENTS

Commonwealth Games steeplechase, finalist, represented NI (Glasgow 2014)

Northern Ireland record holder, 3,000m steeplechase (Oordegem 2014)

Northern Ireland record holder, 5,000m (Manchester 2011)

Northern Ireland record holder, 3,000m (Slovakia 2009)

Irish Champion 3,000m steeplechase (2011)

Irish Indoor Champion 3,000m (2011)

European Team Championships, represented Ireland at the 3,000m steeplechase (Estonia 2014), 5,000m (Dublin 2012) & 3,000m (Budapest 2010 & Slovakia 2009)

European Cross-country Championships, represented Ireland (Slovenia 2011, Portugal 2010 & Belgium 2008)

CAROLINE O'HANLON
NETBALL & GAELIC FOOTBALL

How I first became involved in sport

I was born and reared in rural South Armagh and my father was heavily involved with the local Gaelic Athletic Association club. His idea of babysitting was to take me to the club while he fixed something, took a training session or attended a meeting. So I was engrossed in this environment for as long as I can remember. I came through the club, playing with the boys at underage and then on through the ranks right up until now.

Alongside this, whilst at primary school, I had my first exposure to netball. One of the teachers, Tom McGuinness, had spent many years working in England where netball was a big sport even then, and he had a great passion for the game. My mum also taught in the school so while I was waiting for her to finish work he allowed me to join in training with the older girls. I started when I was seven or eight years old.

Tom had a massive influence on me. I remember him talking about games, and watching videos of matches in which NI were playing, which he had let me borrow. I also remember he had a girl come in who had played for NI and she spoke to us. I remember thinking, 'I want to do that'.

When I went on to Sacred Heart School in Newry, I continued to play both sports. Later I studied medicine at Queen's University, Belfast and they were a great support to me over the years, providing bursaries, training/medical and mentoring services.

Inspiration

Growing up, I was heavily influenced by men's Gaelic Football. My parents would have taken me to all the Carrickcruppen and Armagh matches, and through the late 1990s and 2000s the success of the Armagh team was an inspiration to the county. It was amazing to see the influence sport can have on the entire community – the mood was great, people were buoyant, the excitement was palpable, and anything that stood still was painted orange and white. The pride in the team, and how that filtered down to the people in the streets, was amazing.

There were very few female role models, so iconic figures like Mary Peters and Sonia O'Sullivan were trailblazers. Their achievements have transcended generations. I was lucky enough to have been a recipient of bursaries from the Mary Peters Trust whilst at school and, through that, to hear more of her story. It didn't matter about religion, gender or whatever, her achievements were

universally and globally acknowledged, and she did this during some of NI's darkest days. However, what I admire most about Mary is her endless energy and enthusiasm, always a friendly voice with welcome words of support and encouragement. I love that she is continually finding new challenges. There are not too many people approaching their 80th birthday who would abseil down the sides of buildings. Brilliant! She is a true ambassador and inspiration for sport.

Team sport is a special thing – the commitment, the sacrifices, the compromises that have to made for success can be tough. To always have that feeling of accountability and responsibility to so many others can be hard, but equally can bring out the best in you. There is nothing that beats that feeling of having come through tough times together and sharing the success!

Memories

The pinnacle of my netball career to date has been captaining the NI team. Over the last two years, we have had our most successful period in Netball NI's history – silver medalists at European championships, World Cup 2019 qualification and then the Commonwealth Games in Gold Coast – finishing 8th. Particular highlight at the latter was being ⇒

selected as flag bearer for the opening ceremony. This was a surreal moment for me. I was very shocked as there were other very talented, high-profile athletes in the party, but it really demonstrated for me how highly they valued me as an individual and viewed the sport of netball. When I was asked, I didn't hesitate in accepting.

There were a few negative comments on social media re politics and the flag etc. but they were irrelevant to me. I have chosen to represent NI and am very proud every time I do so. I was overwhelmed by the support I received, particularly locally, and it shows how far the country has come. There is still a small minority of negative voices, but by and large we support each other and are proud to see our own doing well.

Walking out into the stadium in Brisbane, in front of a full house, is a memory that will live long with me. Leading this group, with my friends and teammates who I have played with for more than 10 years by my side, was a very special moment. It really filled me with confidence going into the tournament.

What I am doing now

Netball: I am currently captain of the NI team, and competed in the World Cup in Liverpool in July 2019. I am also playing semi-professional netball in the UK Vitality Superleague, for the champions, Manchester Thunder. Domestically, I am captain of Larkfield Netball Club and we are top of the league and defending champions in the NI Shield.

Football: I am still playing for Armagh in the National Football League and senior championship. I also play for my local club, Carrickcruppen GFC, and we are current Armagh champions. I recently represented Ulster for a 13th year and we were runners-up in the All-Ireland tournament.

ACHIEVEMENTS
Netball

100 senior caps for Northern Ireland, a record

Participated at three World Cups & two Commonwealth Games

Current NI captain, with the team ranked 8th in the world, its highest-ever standing

Gold medal at U21 European Championships

Gaelic football

Record number of appearances for Armagh Ladies

Played at senior level for 19 years, winning three senior Ulster championships

All-Ireland Players' Player of the Year on two occasions

Represented Ulster for 13 years – winning eight All-Ireland titles

***Belfast Telegraph* Sportswoman of the Year**

ATHLETICS

SONIA O'SULLIVAN

How I first became involved in sport

I got started mainly through school. I enjoyed running, even as a young child, and found I was quite good, particularly at long-distance cross-country events. The facilities in Cobh (County Cork) where I was born were limited – almost non-existent in fact – and I didn't run on a track of any kind until I was 12. Even then, I found the distances in which we were allowed to compete too short. The cross-country distances were better, I won my first race, and that is what I concentrated on.

Inspiration

One of my first inspirations was an event called the Community Games. These were held in Mosney Holiday Centre in Co. Meath, and children from all over Ireland would go there to take part in various competitions. If you qualified for them it was a really big deal! It was a huge incentive to perform well in your own county.

When I knew I wanted to take my running really seriously, I decided I needed a trainer and found a very good one – by looking up his name in a telephone book!

Two athletes who inspired me were Marcus O'Sullivan and Frank O'Mara because they performed so brilliantly

for Ireland in tough international competition. Marcus won three World Indoor Championship gold medals at 1500m, and ran a sub four-minute mile on more than 100 occasions during his career. Frank was also an indoor gold medallist on two occasions at 3,000m, including 1987 in America, where Marcus was also victorious.

Memories

Long-distance running is a very individual challenge, but I always loved being part of a team – a group of competitors in different disciplines. I was particularly aware of this when I went to the Olympic Games in Barcelona in 1992. I always enjoyed warm weather training too, and ran well when I was at business school in the USA – breaking the World record for 1500m indoors in Boston in 1991.

Another of the things that really helped my success was something I did when travelling around Europe for track races throughout the summer. I would always run back to the hotel from the stadium after each race, which helped maintain stamina and endurance. It sometimes felt more important than the race itself, having worked out the best route back to hotels in unfamiliar cities all over Europe, and I would try to recruit other athletes to run with me. More often than not we would get back before the official athletes' bus which we always regarded as a victory! The best was after a track meet in Nice when all the athletes' managers organised a fast run back over five miles – just a little bit of pressure on all the runners to keep up – and then a jump in the sea to cool down. The big thing with this exercise was the fun and camaraderie that it created and a relaxed environment when travelling. The athletes were able to deliver results because they were enjoying even more what they were doing while going from race to race.

We also used to gather together and have some tea and biscuits while whiling away the hours. I used to bring the travel kettle, Marcus O'Sullivan had a selection of tea bags and Frank O'Mara the biscuits, and we used to invite athletes from other countries such as the US, GB and Australia to join us. The social aspect of this was vital to ensuring that a tough travelling lifestyle was sustainable. We had many laughs and good memories and these were some of the best times I had while racing and training away from home.

What I am doing now

My husband Nic is an Australian sportsman, so his country has become an important part of my life. I applied for dual citizenship (Ireland/Australia) in 2006 and hoped to run for Australia in the 5,000m at that year's Commonwealth Games in Melbourne, but was injured. We have two daughters, one of whom – Sophie – is proving a good middle-distance runner in her own right. She won a silver medal (800m) at the European U18 Championships in Hungary last year, and I love to watch her and see her doing well.

I still run regularly, and also cycle and swim. I write for an Irish newspaper, and co-commentate on athletics for RTE (TV) in Ireland.

ACHIEVEMENTS

Olympic Games silver medal, 5,000m (Sydney 2000)

World Championships gold medal, 5,000m (Gothenburg 1995) & silver medal, 1500m (Stuttgart 1993)

European Championships gold medals, 3,000m (Helsinki 1994), 5,000m & 10,000m (Budapest 1998) & silver medals, 5,000m & 10,000m (Munich 2002)

World Cross-country champion, 8km & 4km (Marrakesh 1998)

World Indoor gold medal, 3,000m (Paris 1997)

Chef de Mission for Team Ireland at the Olympic Games (London 2012)

Plinth reads ...
Sonia O'Sullivan
International Athlete and Local Hero
Erected by the people of Cobh

Sonia O'Sullivan

ATHLETICS
CHRISTINE OHURUOGU MBE

How I first became involved in sport

I enjoyed any activity when I was growing up, from riding bikes to playing football with my brother and his friends. I did anything and everything as long as it involved running around! It was in school that I began to be involved in sport at a formal level, playing netball, hockey, tennis, rounders and trampolining. However, my first love was netball and I progressed from playing for the school team right through to the England squad. It was only agreeing to fill a gap in the 800m at my school sports day that opened up the avenue of athletics to me.

Inspiration

I have been fortunate to find inspiration from different avenues and often in the most ordinary, everyday occurrences with ordinary people. Growing up, I can recall numerous teachers who encouraged a love of learning and instilled a quiet confidence in me. I was not a particularly confident child growing up, but I can recall many occasions when I was almost ordered to excel and grow and not hold myself back. Simple words of kindness, reassurance and support helped me to dream, and opened up a world in which I could set huge goals.

In sport I was always fortunate to have good coaches who recognised then nurtured my talent. I never grew up watching much TV as I was always too busy for it – playing sport or doing homework. It meant that the people I met daily provided the biggest sources of inspiration and encouragement for me as I grew up.

As for my time in athletics, my main inspiration comes from the fact that I am aware that I have a special talent and I really want to do the best that I can with it. I want to use my time wisely to take my passion for sport as far as I can in the hope of encouraging others to make the most of their talents and to do the same.

Memories

My fondest memory is winning the World Championships in 2013. Not just because I won the race but also because this is when I broke the British Record, which was a goal I'd had for a long time, and the moment when I executed my plan exactly as I wanted.

I am very proud of how I performed in my home Olympics of 2012 where, despite a difficult build-up, I still managed to come away with the silver medal.

A painful memory would be when I false-started at the World Championships in 2011, following which I really questioned my future in the sport. It was not the preparation I had anticipated going into the Olympics in London the year later. I had strong doubts as to whether I could get back to the form that I had displayed in Beijing 2008. However, given time and discussion with those close to me I was able to gather myself to go again.

What I am doing now

I retired from competitive athletics and studied for a Law Degree with a strong emphasis on sporting law. This is my focus after my career as an athlete.

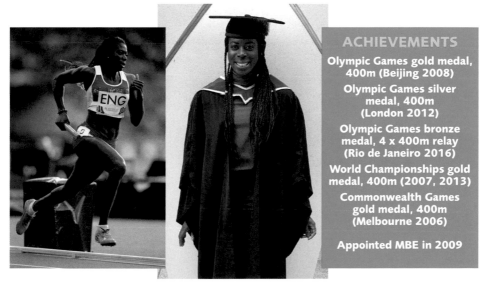

ACHIEVEMENTS

Olympic Games gold medal, 400m (Beijing 2008)

Olympic Games silver medal, 400m (London 2012)

Olympic Games bronze medal, 4 x 400m relay (Rio de Janeiro 2016)

World Championships gold medal, 400m (2007, 2013)

Commonwealth Games gold medal, 400m (Melbourne 2006)

Appointed MBE in 2009

ATHLETICS

ABI OYEPITAN

How I first became involved in sport

I had great teachers who loved sport. One in particular, Mr Dewitt, saw some talent in me for athletics and really pushed me to pursue it. He was the one who persuaded my very strict African parents to allow me to join an athletics club. My parents were not keen – they thought it would distract me from my schoolwork.

Inspiration

The first time I watched athletics on TV was the Barcelona Olympics in 1992. My parents sat us down to watch

> "With Dave I learned mental toughness, I learned how to come back when you lose, and I used to lose a lot!"

Linford Christie in the 100m final, and I remember the roar that came from them when he won the Olympic gold. I remember thinking, 'I want to do that, I want to win an Olympic gold medal.' That really sparked something in me, it always stuck with me, It was an image that drove me throughout my career.

I was really fortunate throughout my career to be surrounded by amazing

people who encouraged and believed in me. The two main inspirations were the two coaches I had. The first was Dave Johnson, who coached me from my early teens until I was 20. Dave was the one that got me to stay in the sport when I could easily have dropped out. He was one of those volunteer coaches who was passionate about athletics. He lived and breathed the sport, and that passion couldn't help but rub off on me. I was a young scrawny 13 year-old kid who turned up at the track one day to find a coach, and he transformed me into a national champion.

The second coach was Tony Lester. He championed me when nobody else would, and his belief in me was unwavering. If Dave taught me the basics about my sport, Tony taught me the rest. With Dave I learned mental toughness, I learned how to come back when you lose, and I used to lose a lot! With Tony, I learned I can truly achieve anything I put my mind to, and went from being a national champion to being a world-class athlete.

Memories

One of the most painful experiences was learning that I would have to have a third operation. I had already had two previous ops on a non-healing stress fracture and hadn't competed properly for nearly five years. Hearing that I needed yet another was truly devastating. It was the first time I really considered giving up the sport. I remember going to Tony to say I was

ACHIEVEMENTS

Olympic Games finalist 200m (Athens 2004)

Olympic Games qualified for 100 & 200m (London 2012)

Commonwealth Games gold medal 4 x 100m relay, silver medal 200m (Delhi 2010)

thinking of retiring and he gave me all the reasons I shouldn't – convincing me to give it one more year and try and make the Commonwealth team. If I didn't then I would have at least done all I could.

So I did what he suggested. I recovered from my injury, went back into training and came back to compete properly for the first time in six years. Not only did I make the Commonwealth team, I won a gold and silver medal and shocked a few people along the way.

I was known to swear a lot through the finishing line when racing. I was always very hard on myself and if it was a close finish or I wasn't happy with the race (which was most of the time) I would swear through the line. Anyway, when they showed the replays of my races, nine times out of 10 you could see me mouthing some kind of swear word. Must have been shocking for lip readers!

What I am doing now

I own a natural skincare line called LIHA Beauty. This is worlds away from sport but it keeps me busy.

ATHLETICS

JO PAVEY MBE

How I first became involved in sport

I always loved being active as a child. I spent hours bike riding, roller-skating and playing football with the boys on the street. At primary school, it wasn't obvious that I could be a runner. At sports day, I never did that well as we only did 60-70m sprints.

It wasn't until I went to secondary school that I got the chance to run longer distances. One afternoon, our PE teacher asked us to run two laps of the school grass track. She was pleased with how I did, and recommended that I go to an athletics club. A family friend who took her own sons to Exeter Harriers AC kindly offered to take me along. After trying many events, I joined a group that specialised in distance running, and things went from there.

I suppose I got involved in sport because I have always loved setting myself a challenge or a goal to aim for. It's fun working towards goals and monitoring your progress. Sport boosts how you feel and makes you feel more able to embrace other challenges in life. Also, from a young age, I really enjoyed the camaraderie of being part of a team, and I still love it today.

Inspiration

I remember watching the Olympics when I was a schoolgirl and being amazed by the performances of athletes such as Steve Cram and Wendy Sly. I was also greatly impressed by Liz McColgan winning the World Championships in Tokyo in 1991.

I was also inspired by Mary Peters and I love watching the footage of when she won her Olympic gold in 1972. I admire her for her great achievements and determination. I also love the way she embraced the true spirit of sport with her smiling face, and the support of her fellow competitors during events was lovely to see. She is a fantastic role model.

Memories

I was at a televised Grand Prix meeting in Gateshead to race in the 3,000m. My good friend Kelly Holmes was going to compete in the 800m. However, she had no spikes to race in as her bag had gone missing from her flight. She had managed to get some running kit, but no running spikes. Luckily we had the same size feet so I said she could borrow mine. The only difficulty was that her race was the one immediately after mine. I therefore had to panic to take my spikes off as soon as I crossed the line. Kelly just about managed to get them on in time to line up for her race. She ran a very speedy time of 1min 58.10secs. I joked with her afterwards that it was the fastest a pair of my spikes will ever run!

What I am doing now

I took a break after taking part in my 5th Olympics in Rio. I'm obviously getting on a bit in age now in athletics terms – being 45, but I have no plans to retire yet. I'm a mum of two young children, Jacob and Emily, and it's busy juggling my training around the kids, but my husband Gavin – who is also my coach – is very supportive. I also enjoy being able to go training together as a family. It's nice to be able to show the kids that it's fun to be active. I would like to continue to race on the track but I would also like to do more road racing in the next couple of years, and even have my eyes on the Tokyo Olympics in 2020!

ACHIEVEMENTS

Olympic Games 5th 5,000m (Greece 2004)

World Championships bronze medal 10,000m (Osaka 2007)

European Championships gold medal, 10,000m (Zurich 2014)

European Championships silver medal, 10,000m (Helsinki 2012)

Commonwealth Games bronze medal, 5,000m (Glasgow 2014)

Commonwealth Games silver medal, 5,000m (Melbourne 2006)

Appointed MBE in 2015

PAULINE PEEL (NÉE BIRD THEN HART)

How I first became involved in sport

My father was a disabled athlete (cyclist, swimmer and rower) who inspired me to get involved in sport and acted as my coach. He provided the ambition initially and I joined the senior women's national rowing squad at the age of 16. The 'crunch' moment, when I found my own ambition, was in 1976 when the national coach told me that I was unlikely to make the Olympic team. I found that I really, really wanted to go to the Olympics in Montreal and would move heaven and earth to do it. Actually, that moment was absolutely life-changing – from being a fairly easy-going type of teenager I suddenly found the will to drive myself on to achieve things and this proved useful to the present day.

Inspiration

My father was very keen that my brother and I should be involved in sport – so there really wasn't much choice! However, I have continued to row, competing at Masters championships, and am now involved in cycling because I developed a love of sport for its own sake. I was especially pleased to be able to put something back as a Games maker in 2012 (I marshalled the mountain bike racing) which was possibly more inspiring than competing myself.

> ## ACHIEVEMENTS
> **Individual & Team**
> **Olympic Games competitor
> (Montreal 1976 & Moscow 1980)**
> **World Rowing Championships competitor
> (1977–1979)**
> **Commonwealth Games silver medals, coxless
> pairs & coxed eights (Edinburgh 1986)**

I was also inspired, at my first World Rowing Championships, by the perfection of some of the Eastern Bloc crews, especially the East German women's quadruple scull. It was probably the result of a lot of very boring training sessions working on the sort of marginal gains that would be familiar to David Brailsford, but the precision of their timing (very difficult to achieve) was awe-inspiring … and nothing to do with drugs.

Memories

I race against some of the former Eastern Bloc girls at Masters Championships now and I am saddened that they seem to avoid those of us they used to race in the bad old days. I suppose they were embarrassed about the drugs scandals, but I want to say, 'It's OK, I know it was just the system' and in the past few years I have at least managed to achieve nodding and smiling terms with some of them. That makes me happy. After all, we're just athletes, doing the sport that we love and it's great that we can compete on a level footing now.

ATHLETICS

LADY MARY PETERS LG

How I first became involved in sport

As a child I lived in Heywood, Liverpool, and used to play outside with my brother and two of his friends. There were no girls other than me in our road so I was a bit of a tomboy. There was a farm nearby, so we were always playing in the fields, jumping ditches, climbing trees, playing rounders – and on our birthdays my mother Hilda would organise races in the cornfields.

I always felt challenged to be better than my brother who was three years older than me. When the corn was cut, the stubble could be quite spikey so I ran even faster than usual because I didn't like the feeling of it! But I enjoyed the sensation of being physically energetic and was happy to show it. I must have been quite self-aware. I would skip in the driveway so that people going past would see this active youngster. I used to wash the front doorstep to our house for my mum and hoped that anyone passing by would think, 'Here is a good little girl'.

When we moved to Ballymena in Northern Ireland, I was suddenly the big girl, even though I was always called 'the wee girl'. There we played cricket and I did a bit of hockey. I still wasn't really involved in athletics because, for some reason, at Ballymena Academy it was an activity for the 4th Year up. But I used to go and watch, and loved seeing people compete and do their best. On the estate where we lived, there was a patch of ground with a hut where a workman used to keep his tools. I don't know why, but I dug a pit and riddled the soil so I could run and jump into it. I had done a little bit of long jumping in Liverpool on School Sports Day, but I had never seen anyone doing it really seriously. But this was a start.

⟹

Inspiration

When I was 14 we moved to Portadown, where the headmaster Donald Woodman encouraged every pupil in the school to do some sport. We had a House system, and through competition you could score points for your House, which was very important. So we would do every sport. I wasn't good at anything to begin with – I didn't have an eye for a ball – and even though I played hockey, I was positioned at the back, probably because I was stronger than most. I had trials but didn't get on a school team. As for netball, I just played badly.

The turning point came when I was trying to play cricket one day. Mr Woodman approached me and said: 'There's an athletics coach in the next field and I'd like you to come and meet him.' This was Kenneth McClelland, a former pupil, who was doing some coaching with the boys. I was allowed to join in, and Kenneth encouraged me to try all sorts of athletic events.

At school we just did the 100yds, 220yds, high jump and long jump, but when I was 16, Kenneth asked me if I would like to try a pentathlon. I had no idea what a pentathlon was, but was told I had to learn the two new skills of hurdling and putting the shot. So my dad Arthur, who had already provided me with a high jump pit in the field behind our house with a load of sand, made me a set of hurdles. Because I wanted to practise the shot, dad got me a ton of cement for my 17th birthday and made me a circle next to the high jump pit, and got a stop board made.

I started breaking the Northern Ireland record very quickly, but every time they weighed my shot – as they were required to do – it came in a little bit under. So dad went to a foundry and got one made which was precisely the correct poundage. This was really helpful to the challenge of the pentathlon. I took to it like a duck to water. I had speed but I wasn't very mobile so I had to do a lot of exercises to loosen me up. I had fallen in love with athletics and dad would drive us anywhere in Northern Ireland for an event that was going on. I used to come home with prizes for my mum, which I loved.

As athletics became a much more significant part of my life, I began to appreciate the competition, the travel and the friendship. There were two star athletes in NI at the time. One was Thelma Hopkins, an international hockey player and athlete, and Maeve Kyle, who was also a hockey international and a 400m runner, and they were to become my great friends. They were both very inspiring but, to begin with, we thought sport was fun rather than serious. We were all amateurs. We didn't do it for any reward. Representing your country, and the pride you felt was what mattered, and the opportunities it gave you.

Early achievements

I came third in my first pentathlon and dad decided that I should go to the British Championships in Birmingham. I won the silver medal, and that was when people really began to notice my ability and give me encouragement.

I went to the Empire Games in Cardiff in 1958, representing Northern Ireland, and as members of a team we were given matching blazers, which I loved. We were required to buy our own grey skirt to go with it, which I duly did. However, when I rang our team manager to say that I had bought my skirt, I left it in the phone box by mistake. When I went back, it had gone. I was very upset. I had little money in my Post Office account, but I had to go out and buy another one. At the time, it was quite traumatic!

I was invited to join Spartan Ladies Athletics Club, with which Maria Hartman, the British Team Manager, was involved. They were going to the Netherlands for a club meet and they invited me to go along. So I joined the club and we had a fabulous time. More importantly, I put the shot really well and that gave me the opportunity for my first international match, against Germany at the White City. To be honest, I would rather have been doing any event other than the shot, but not many women were competing in it at the time so I seized my chance.

A year later was the Commonwealth Games in Perth, Australia. What a wonderful opportunity to travel and compete! People weren't travelling far in those days, but my brother had emigrated to Australia so it was an opportunity for me to go and see him as well. I met Mary Rand who was not only absolutely beautiful but also a really talented athlete. There was a coach called Dennis Watts, who also coached Ann Packer. Apart from the fact that she was also very beautiful, she had great natural talent whereas I had to work at it. But we had great fun and I loved being with both of them.

Memories

My mum passed away from cancer when I was 16 and, as devastating as this was for the family, I still wanted to carry on with my athletics, for her. Dad married my godmother within six months of mum's death and that proved a testing time for a young girl. I did sport more to get away from the house, which I saw as a transition of necessity. I did love my stepmother, but found it very difficult to see her being given things that my mother had always wanted, such as a washing machine and a fridge.

Even after she had passed away, I wanted to feel that my mother would have been proud of my achievements. I know my dad was very proud of me too, but he could never put his arms around me and give me a cuddle, which is what I wanted most. He'd had a rough start in life, and had to work hard for everything, but I think I reminded him of my mum too much. He could never show any emotion to me.

I remember that the last time I saw him in Australia, before he died, he said: 'The worst day of my life was when my wife Hilda died' and I recall saying, 'But you have to remember, dad, that she was my mum too ...' The headmaster was kinder to me because he was more understanding. Dad gave me education and opportunities, but I would have loved him to show me more affection. That's why sharing my success with so many people now means so much to me. I hope I am showing them my love.

Major competitions

When I had become very competitive and successful, I disappointed my coach Buster McShane by only winning a silver medal at the Commonwealth Games in Jamaica in 1966. He had encouraged me to gain 2st in weight, which certainly wasn't popular with me. There was no pentathlon at that time, so the shot was my target. Unfortunately, the men's decathlon was cutting across the shot circle where we were trying to compete that evening, so they delayed our event for an hour, by which time I had lost the concentration and drive I had built up. Val Young, an athlete from New Zealand who had come out from retirement, beat me on the night, and my coach Buster McShane was fuming. He stormed away and wouldn't speak to me. He thought I'd thrown away an opportunity. When he was persuaded to return by the team manager, I told him: 'Well at least when I go home to Belfast, people will still like me.' He said: 'What a stupid attitude. If that's the way you think you might as well give up sport now' but that was me wanting love again. It was a low point for me, yet an inspiration it itself because the next Commonwealth Games was going to include a pentathlon. I thought I would like to win that AND the shot, which I did. And when I came home, people did still like me.

> "What a stupid attitude. If that's the way you think you might as well give up sport now"

Sharing the two gold medals with everyone made me realize for the first time that I did have the ability and made me believe that, if I set my mind to it, I could win the Olympic gold.

In September 1971, a year before the Olympics, we went to Crystal Palace and watched everyone do this new style of high jumping called the Fosbury Flop. At the end of the session, Buster told me to get my athletics kit on and we'd go and try it. Because I had strong legs and strong vertical drive I jumped higher than I'd ever jumped before. I realized then that that was going to be a benefit. Also, my hurdles were coming on and I was doing fast times. But I was never going to be a great sprinter because I had such a short stride. When people asked me why I didn't lengthen it I had to admit that I had been trying for 25 years without success!

I enjoyed that year of hard, hard work and everything was geared mentally and physically towards Munich. I was fortunate to win a Churchill Scholarship to America for ⇒

six weeks which not only meant I could train in the sunshine, which was great, but also meant I didn't have to work full-time as well. I had a multitude of tracks I could train on, and stayed with a friend of Buster's called Bill Pearl who was a former Mister Universe.

I began lifting and squatting huge weights and really building strength both physically and mentally. But I over-trained, because I had all day to do it, and eventually strained an Achilles tendon. The problem turned out to be a new pair of trainers which were tight and rubbing, so I threw those away and got some new ones. Even so I feared my Olympic dream could be over.

Fortunately, I recovered from that setback. When I returned to Britain, I went to an event at the Highland Games in Edinburgh and did 5ft 10ins in the high jump. Normally my best would be 5ft 7ins, so with the shot and hurdles going well too it meant a big points improvement for the pentathlon. I had also done a lot of sprint training in America on synthetic tracks – similar to what I would face in Munich – and that helped too.

The Olympic dream

When I went to the Olympics in 1972 I was 33, a mature woman, still doing what I had always really enjoyed but now with a fierce desire to succeed, which hadn't always been the case. I feared the challenge of West German Heide Rosendahl, who I already knew well, because she was such a good long jumper and sprinter, but not the East German, Burglinde Pollak who I thought looked a bit 'soft' on the eve of the competition.

Even then it wasn't all plain sailing. The officials for the hurdles rejected my spikes which had a new wedge design, and I had to wear a replacement pair. Fortunately, I had trained in the second pair and was familiar with them and, in retrospect I was probably better off using them. It also rained, and there were times when I felt a bit chilly. I was so well prepared, so ready to compete, that I wanted everything to be perfect.

On the morning of the competition, a friend was going to waken me and bring me breakfast to my room in the team village. However, she slept in and it didn't happen. Then the car in which we were going to be driven to the stadium didn't turn up. We saw some Australian competitors in a minibus and tried to thumb a lift, but they just drove on. Not a great start! Eventually we did get a lift to the stadium and warmed up well. Bizarrely, Heide's coach came over and told me that I was favourite for the gold medal. Whether this was supposed to distract me in some way, I don't know, but it actually made feel good and boosted my confidence.

I ran as fast a 100m hurdles as I ever had in a pentathlon, the second fastest time in the competition. Then we had to hang around for the shot put. When we got to the warm-up area, the three West German competitors were missing. They were obviously warming up elsewhere on their own, and thus able to get in many more practice puts than the other 15 of us who had to take it turns. This clearly wasn't fair, so I had them 'fetched' to bring them in line with everyone else. After all, this was the Olympic Games and everyone should be presented with the same opportunity. It wasn't like me to be bitchy, but on this occasion it was self-preservation. I proceeded to put further than I had previously in a pentathlon, which was a long way in comparison with the average of the others taking part.

Then it was back to the village to wait for the high jump, which was in the evening. I had some lunch and tried to relax before returning to the stadium. Of course, the high jump in a pentathlon takes for ever because competitors start at really low heights in order to get some points on the board. I kept trying to lie down and relax – until I saw my coach in a yellow jacket gesticulating wildly for me to get up and warm up. I failed twice at 5ft 7ins and then cleared it at the third attempt – and then went up and up and up until 5ft 11¾ins, by which time most people had left the stadium. But a crowd of British athletes, including Jeffrey Archer, stayed behind and were chanting my name. I came away feeling euphoric as I had done three personal bests, and was way ahead in the competition.

I had a restless night, and the long jump was early the following morning. I did an average distance, just under 20ft, but Heide jumped out of her skin and started closing in on me at the top of the leader board.

Yet again we had to go back to the village and wait for the 200m in the evening. For some reason I thought the best athletes in the competition would be in the first heat whereas, in fact, we were in the final heat. I only discovered this after I had already warmed up. So I just lay down on the high jump mat and relaxed until our time came. Eventually they were ready for us and I went on to the track and put my starting blocks in and tried them out. They slipped and I stumbled. If I hadn't checked them, and it happened in the actual race, I would have been down and out. Thank goodness for proper preparation! When it came to the start of the race, it was amazing that in a crowd of 80,000 I could hear my name being chanted and cheered on by people I knew. Buster had calculated that for me to beat Heide to the gold medal I would have to run faster than ever before, and I recall the fear of losing it in the last race. I did sprint as fast as I could, but there was an interminable wait at the finish line for the results. Remember, there was no computer timing in those days it was all decided by a hand-held stopwatch. Eventually Heide's time went up and it was really fast, then two other athletes, and then mine. Even at that moment I didn't know if I had done enough. Then I saw Heide coming towards me and she gave me a hug and I knew that I had won. The final points difference was just 10 out of 4,800 or, put another way, about a centimetre or one-hundredth of a second. Deep down, I knew it was always meant to be.   ⇒

I was presented with my gold medal by the Marquis of Exeter, a former 400m hurdler, who was a member of the IOC. There was so much euphoria when I came home that it was difficult for my coach to deal with. Everyone wanted a bit of me, but I worked for Buster and I had to go back to the day job. It was a difficult time, but I enjoyed all the honours that came with it – the Sports Personality of the Year, the Athletics Writers and Sports Writers awards.

The night after I won, the British Olympic Association had a party for me. My dad had turned up in Munich, I didn't know he was there, and he had been watching me for the two days. He came to the party and I said to Buster: 'What's going on? I feel there is something happening.' He said: 'Nothing you need to know about.' I insisted, and it turned out that the BBC had received a phone call saying that if I returned to Belfast I would be shot, and that my flat would be bombed. I said immediately that there was no question of my not going home, but my dad had heard about the threat and wanted me to go with him to Australia. Nevertheless, I refused and said I would go home regardless. It was arranged that I would leave early, especially in view of what had happened to the Israeli athletes during the Games. I didn't realize until later that Heide had also had to move out of the Olympic Village because she was Jewish, and had received threats to her life. She went on to win gold in the long jump and as a member of the 400m relay squad, so ours were very parallel experiences. I flew to London and then on to Belfast, and as I was getting off the plane a man tapped me on the shoulder and said: 'My colleague and I are security police – we have been shadowing you all the way home.' Because it was the worst year of the Troubles in Northern Ireland, the public wasn't allowed into the airport building, but there was a band playing 'Congratulations' as I came down the steps, and hundreds of people at the perimeter fence giving me cards and bunches of flowers. A gold Rolls-Royce had also been laid on to take me into Belfast, and the streets were hung with

welcome signs. But even then I was taken on a different route to the one originally planned because there fears for my safety. I went to the gym first, then to lunch at the Belfast Telegraph and was finally taken in an open-topped lorry to meet the Lord Mayor. I remember telling him: 'I went for gold, I won gold and I brought it home for you.' There were more events in the afternoon, a special cake with all the events on at the Europa Hotel, a bracelet gift from UTV, but I still wasn't allowed to go home to my flat on the Antrim Road. I went to

stay with Buster and his family in Cultra, which had its own beach and boathouse, and stayed there for a number of months because they still feared for my life. I really wanted to go home but I couldn't.

Memories

When I was at primary school (in Hunt's Cross, Liverpool) the bus fare was a penny each way. There was a dairy on the way home where, for 1d, you could buy either an Oxo cube or the wafers for an ice cream. No ice cream, just the wafer biscuits. So occasionally I would spend my money there and would run/walk the two miles home. My favourite penny treat was to suck on an Oxo cube, and get very brown teeth as a result. Can you imagine that today? But it was full of nourishment and probably helped give me strength. Remember, it was the war years.

When I first started competing in the shot put, the British champion was Suzanne Allday, who was a smoker. It amused me that when she was called to compete, she would step into the circle and leave her lit cigarette on the edge of the stop board for afterwards!

Years after the Munich Olympics, I met Heide Rosendahl's husband – an American basketball player – in a hotel somewhere in Europe. I said: 'I know who you are ... I bet you don't know who I am.' He replied: 'I bet I do ... how did you beat my wife?' I simply said: 'I needed it more.'

What I am doing now

The Mary Peters Trust, which was set up in 1975, has helped over 4,000 athletes, in the broadest sense of the word. They include surfers, golfers, hockey players, gymnasts, table tennis players, and paralympians, to name just a few, and I get the greatest thrill from watching these young people travelling all over world, representing us and leading healthy, fit lives.

ACHIEVEMENTS

Olympic Games gold medal, pentathlon, (Munich 1972)

Commonwealth Games gold medal, pentathlon, (Christchurch NZ 1974)

Commonwealth Games gold medal, pentathlon, (Edinburgh 1970)

Commonwealth Games gold medal, shot put, (Edinburgh 1970)

Commonwealth Games gold medal, shot put, (Kingston 1966)

Appointed Lady Companion of the Order of the Garter in 2019

Appointed DStJ in 2017

Appointed CH in 2015

Appointed DBE in 2000

Appointed CBE in 1990

Appointed MBE in 1973

BBC Sports Personality of the Year, 1972

Freeman of the cities of Lisburn and Belfast

PAULA RADCLIFFE MBE

How I first became involved in sport

I love running and the feeling and buzz I get from it. Through sport I have shared, experienced and grown so much that it will always be a central part of my life. I want it to be a part of my children's lives too and for them to experience the fun and enjoyment that I had.

Inspiration

My grandmother was a huge inspiration to me. She taught me to have fun always and to realize that you get out of life what you put in; to have the courage to go after your dreams and goals; to try another way each time that you fail, and to always treat others as you would want to be treated yourself. Above all she taught me that family is key and you should always be there for one another.

Within sport, the three 'First Ladies of marathon running'– Grete Waitz, Ingrid Kristiansen and Joan Benoit Samuelson – were inspirational too.

Grete for what she accomplished in running on all three surfaces (road, track and cross-country) but most of all for the amazing person that she was, and for the braveness and dignity with which she fought cancer to the end.

I remember watching Ingrid en route to the women's World record in London, and being inspired to also run that strong, fast and freely one day. She is a lovely, genuine lady who still spends so much time giving back to her sport and encouraging others to be fit.

Joanie was the first women's Olympic champion but, more than that, is such an energetic, friendly and kind lady. It is privilege now to count her also as a friend.

Of course, I must also include my coach Alex Stanton, husband Gary Lough, and all our families, for helping and guiding me to work for my dreams and always being there through good and bad times.

Memories

I have three vivid memories:

1 I once had a marriage proposal at mile 17 of the Chicago Marathon. I didn't accept!

2 A group of Rabbis crossed the road, believing it was a normal Sunday morning in New York as the elite women's marathon field ran by. They were almost knocked over by the camera bikes and escort vehicles.

3 I was arrested for managing to run into an American NATO base in Tirrenia, Italy, while on a World Cross-Country preparation camp in 1999. Bad move! We had no passport or ID on us and were made to re-trace the 10-mile run back to the training camp (although at the time we were within sight of it) to show how we had managed to get in. For the rest of the time we were in the camp, they followed us around in trucks.

ACHIEVEMENTS

World Championships gold medal, marathon (Helsinki 2005)

World Cross-Country champion (2000, 2001) & runner-up (1997, 1998)

World record-holder (marathon & 10km road)

Three World Half Marathon Championship wins (2000, 2001, 2003)

European Championship gold medal, marathon (Munich 2002)

Commonwealth Games gold medal, 5,000m (Manchester, 2002)

London Marathon winner (2002, 2003, 2005)

Chicago Marathon winner (2002)

Appointed MBE in 2002

BBC Sports Personality of the Year, 2002

Inducted into the English Athletics Hall of Fame, 2010

HOCKEY

ALISON RAMSAY

How I first became involved in sport

I used to run 200m and 400m when I was a teenager and enjoyed athletics although knew that I would never have been good enough to compete internationally. I have always been a very competitive and determined (some might say stubborn) individual and I always wanted (and still want) to be the very best I can be at whatever I am doing. I realized that I would never make it to the very top in athletics and also found it a really lonely sport. When I started playing hockey I realized how much more I preferred being part of a team than competing for myself, and I knew that if I worked really hard, and did everything that I could to make the most of my limited hockey skills I could be a much more successful hockey player than an athlete.

Inspiration

I was inspired, and not just on a sporting level, by Martina Navratilova. Her physical and mental toughness and determination to succeed on the tennis court, together with her self-belief and confidence in herself as a person, made her someone I have always admired. I was also inspired by the game of hockey itself. I enjoyed the challenge the sport presented to me and, although not a naturally talented player, I worked very

hard for many years to be the very best I could be.

Memories

When the final whistle blew in our bronze medal game in Barcelona, and I knew it was the last time I would play for GB, I had a mixture of emotions – I was proud of what I had achieved, relieved in a way too that we finally had something tangible to show for the team's efforts and also disbelief that it had actually happened. Standing on the medal rostrum with my team mates with Olympic medals round our necks made all the years of hard work worthwhile.

Back in the 80s hockey was still very much an amateur sport with no Lottery funding, so players had to fund-raise to buy kit and get themselves to tournaments. I remember that we were extremely grateful to receive some free T-shirts sponsored by Outspan oranges, until we actually saw them ... two oranges, and their advertising slogan 'Small ones are more juicy' strategically placed right across our chests!

Also, I remember that in order to get to one European Cup tournament all of the Scotland players and their families had to buy packets and packets of Persil soap powder, as at the time the company was giving away vouchers that entitled you to get two for the price of one rail tickets. We managed to get to the tournament by train and ferry (no money for air fares in those days) and the bonus was we had *really* clean kit too!

I was in a Scotland team that played an away match against Germany in the late 1980s. At the start of the match the national anthems are traditionally played and all started well with the familiar strains of Scotland the Brave being played on the bagpipes over the tannoy to the assembled crowd. Unfortunately, however, our hosts must have acquired a CD (no Spotify in those days) with a medley of well-known Scottish songs that seamlessly merged from one to the next so, before we knew it, we had also been treated to *The Northern Lights of Old Aberdeen* and were halfway through *I Belong To Glasgow* before enough hand gestures were made to let our hosts know that something was amiss!

What I am doing now

I was a late developer as far as hockey was concerned, never being selected at any junior level and only gaining my first cap aged 23, an age at which some players now retire! This is possibly the reason why I am still playing, albeit at a much slower pace, today. If I am speaking to young players who maybe haven't been selected at junior age group levels, I can quite genuinely tell them that they are already much better at hockey than I was at their age. I encourage them not to give up on their dream of playing internationally if that is really what they want to do.

I still enjoy keeping fit, the buzz of competitive sport and the challenge of learning new hockey skills that the youngsters nowadays take for granted. Playing Masters hockey has provided me with international competition but also, importantly, the continued camaraderie of being part of a team with like-minded people.

Like most sportswomen, I had lows in my sporting career and also incredible highs, most notably winning an Olympic medal. That high felt even more special because of the contrast with the low four years before when we were 4th and just failed to medal at the previous Olympic Games. Looking back I have no regrets. I know I did everything I could to make myself the very best hockey player. I believe it is possible to succeed in most sport with great determination and commitment and limited skill but not with great skill and limited determination and commitment. All any of us can do is strive to play the sport we love to the very best of our ability and if my story inspires others to do this then that would be fantastic.

ACHIEVEMENTS

Olympic bronze medal Team GB (Barcelona 1992)

259 international hockey caps (150 for Scotland & 109 for GB): a World record at the time of retirement from international hockey (1995) & acknowledged in the *Guinness Book of Records*

First female player to reach 100 international GB caps

143

KATE RICHARDSON-WALSH OBE

How I first became involved in sport

My parents were both PE teachers and loved sport, so my sister Rachel and I had a go at most activities. I did a lot of gymnastics and swimming as a youngster, and when I went to my local secondary school we played hockey, netball and athletics. My PE teacher was a really enthusiastic hockey player, as was my mum, and they passed their passion on to me. I immediately fell in love with the team aspect of hockey and felt I'd found a place in which I belonged.

Inspiration

Growing up, there weren't so many female athletes shown on TV on a regular basis. My role models, therefore, came around every four years when the Olympic Games were taking place. The Barcelona 1992 games were the first that I remember clearly. Sally Gunnell won gold in the 400m hurdles and the GB women's hockey team won bronze. The pictures of those women standing proudly on that Olympic podium were just dream-like to me as a 12 year-old girl. I just remember thinking, 'Wow, those women are amazing!'

Strangely, getting dropped from the Junior England team, aged 15, was a pivotal point in my life, and therefore inspirational in a way. I was at a crossroads in my life and I needed to make some big choices about what I wanted to do. Although being a professional hockey player wasn't an option when I was growing up, I decided to be the best hockey player I could, and tried to keep that mindset for the rest of my career. There have been many occasions in my sporting career where devastation or failure has kick-started a new path.

ACHIEVEMENTS

Olympic Games gold medal, Team GB (Rio 2016)
Olympic Games bronze medal (London 2012)
Most-capped British female hockey player (375 appearances)
My wife Helen & I were the first same-sex, married couple to win Olympic Gold together

Appointed OBE in 2017
Appointed MBE in 2015

Memories

I feel so very lucky to have been invited to attend many incredible events and functions as a result of being an international hockey player. One such occasion was an invitation to Helen and I to The Queen's State Banquet at Buckingham Palace for the King and Queen of the Netherlands. Having never had an occasion to wear our MBE and OBE medals we were thrilled to be getting them out of the boxes! We had ignored the advice on purchasing a smaller commemorative medal because ... well, we thought we'd never wear it to be honest. So we rolled up to Buckingham Palace, driving my dirty white Kia Rio into the Buckingham Palace courtyard, wearing our enormous blingy Honours medals and (frankly) sticking out like a sore thumb. The only thing that topped all of this was seeing the absolute horror on the faces of the King and Queen of the Netherlands when we were introduced during the evening. They couldn't quite believe that the Royal Family had very cheekily rubbed their noses in losing out on 'their' Dutch hockey gold! Suffice to say, I'm not sure we'll be invited back!

What I am doing now

I am now coaching at Hampstead & Westminster HC with Sarah Kelleher. I hope to develop my coaching over the coming years. I also visit schools around the country, coaching hockey and hopefully inspiring the next generation to pursue their dreams. I also get to do some punditry and commentary for hockey as it is now shown more regularly on TV. I am a patron of the Women's Sport Trust and Access Sport, and co-chair of the International Hockey Federation (FIH) Athletes' Commission.

SHIRLEY ROBERTSON OBE

How I first became involved in sport

I have never been renowned for my athletic abilities. Running, throwing, catching or doing something elegant on a mat was not really my thing. But I loved to be outside, was undoubtedly a competitive child and, looking back, fairly tenacious. The adventure really began when I was seven, when my father built a kit boat in the garage (it was the late 70s and DIY was all the rage). I raced with him at a family club on a loch in the Trossachs in Scotland and, when I was 12, the club started cadet training. With a little encouragement my eyes were opened. I could sail on my own, way better than my dad quite quickly, and I wanted to get even better and better. I loved the independence and thought there was always so much to learn, to improve ... and there still is!

Inspiration

Growing up in Scotland we had some really strong women sports stars. I'll never forget watching Liz McColgan run with a broken foot and the fortitude of Yvonne Murray. I admired that kind of grit and often felt the harder things got, the more I came into my own. I love a good storm! In the world of sailing my inspiration has to be Tracy Edwards, even though she wasn't in the Olympic arena. In the 80s and 90s she almost singlehandedly put women's sailing on the map. She was not, in herself, an extraordinary offshore sailor but she always believed she could make things happen. She was ambitious and not put off by the naysayers, and when she had to make hard decisions she backed herself. I often thought of her attitude when it was tough, and still do.

Memories

My greatest achievement was not giving up after my 4th place at the Atlanta Olympics and 'rebooting' my approach to delivering when it mattered. I had been inconsolable, properly broken-hearted immediately after the Games, and I didn't know where to turn or what to do. I remember flying home and just sitting in my car at Gatwick Airport for hours. However, admitting my mistakes honestly, not just in the competition but also my shortcomings in my preparation and attitude, led to me to win gold four years later in Sydney. Mine was a 'no stone left unturned' approach, and taking more ownership of the process put me in solid medal contention. I finally felt like I had fully taken it on, I had stopped 'playing' at it.

Another four years later (Athens, 2004), and still with a 'Golden Glow', I arrogantly assumed I could take on a new challenge, this time a team event – a three-woman boat. With 18 months to go, we had no money, no race boat, no coach and were missing a crew member, it wasn't looking like the polished winning outfit I was used to! Securing a good coach, and adopting a relentless schedule of training in the Olympic venue combined with equipment development, left us unstoppable come Games time, winning easily. I remember the medal ceremony so vividly. It felt such a massive relief, especially for my two young crewmates – a real vindication of the tough decisions that had to be made and our relentless work ethic.

The best moments, obviously, are winning Olympic medals. Hearing the first notes of our national anthem still gives me shivers. But I also remember vividly one of my teammates in Athens, sitting crumpled in a ball in the tunnel waiting for our medal turn. It was simply the very moment it had finally sunk in — we'd done it!

The most difficult moment was trying for one more gold medal at the Beijing Games, just after having twins. In hindsight it was a crazy time. I was up all night with babies, training all day, and was pretty unsupported. In the end, I narrowly missed out on selection due to a couple of poor decisions. Perhaps you can't have it all!

What I am doing now

I have worked in broadcasting for the last 14 years and have sailed faster, bigger boats than I did at the Games. I've had some crazy opportunities, including driving a £30 million super yacht against 20 other multi-million pound super yachts. It's somewhat different from sailing a little dinghy in the Trossachs of Scotland! I'm fascinated by people and how they work under pressure. I know what it means to athletes to win or lose. I'll still watch any sport with a lot at stake, but sailing is my passion, it's a really diverse sport, packed with crazy diverse characters, and the story-telling opportunities are endless.

ACHIEVEMENTS

Olympic gold medal, Europe class (Sydney 2000)
Olympic gold medal, Yngling class (Athens 2004)
World Championship silver medals, Europe class
(Kalovig 1993, Travemunde 1998 & Salvador da Bahia 2000)

Appointed OBE in 2005
Appointed MBE in 2000
Female Sailor of the Year 2000

NETBALL

LIZ RODGERS

6TH WORLD NETBALL TOURNAMENT
SINGAPORE JUNE 11TH–24TH 1983

How I first became involved in sport

I always had an interest in exercise and an aptitude for it, even from a young age. I was constantly on the go – I walked, or ran, everywhere because we had no family car. I loved to run, jump, skip and roller skate, and even had to slow down occasionally during games of chase to let the boys catch me! We played hopscotch, and games we knew as two-ball, German skipping, kerbie and street tennis ... in fact, a lot of street activities because it was safe to play outside on our council housing estate in those days. At the time it wouldn't have seemed like it was the starting point for the high-level competitive sport and international representation to come, but I guess it was.

Inspiration

It is so important to acknowledge and thank the people who were instrumental in helping to develop my early sporting interests and achievements – especially those who are not internationally-known names. One of my PE teachers at Wallace High School in Lisburn, Joan Gough, was a big influence, and a French teacher, Betty Totten, encouraged me and my best friend to go for schoolgirl and county trials. After school, I went to the Ulster College of Physical Education, which was the best time of my life! Influential lecturers there were Roy Downey, Moya Gibson and Ann Curran, all of whom helped launch me into my own teaching career, which I loved. Also I remember with affection my squad coaches at various age levels of representation – Norma Gamble, Maureen Mawhinney, Sheelagh O'Prey, Mary French and Mary Hicks. Some became my lifelong friends too.

Among international stars, I loved to watch Bjorn Borg play tennis. I was impressed by his cool demeanour and athleticism, and how long he played the game. I enjoy seeing Andy Murray and Rafael Nadal too. I also love athletics, and I think I was a little in love with Colin Jackson ... he was the full package! I always enjoyed Daley Thompson's cheeky antics, as well as his supreme talent, and Mary Peters was simply amazing. That a girl from Northern Ireland could take on the world in pentathlon and succeed was fabulous ... especially in that era.

Memories

Another of my PE teachers at high school, Eric Greene, was good fun and a big influence on my love of sport. I recall he played a wee prank on me by filling up my hockey bag with rocks when we were preparing to leave for a sports tour to Chester, so that when we came to depart I couldn't lift it on to the team bus. He always called me Lonnie, because my maiden name was Donegan ... and it stuck.

At the start of our tournament in Singapore in 1983, word went around that we were to be genetically tested for our 'femininity'. Inevitably, rumours spread and Kate Leonard, our team manager, made us all very anxious with her assertion that our nether regions would come under extremely close scrutiny. Sweating profusely on our way into the medical room, we were mightily relieved to find out that it was only a saliva test. Phew!! I still have the certificate to prove that I'm female ... yeay!

What I am doing now

I play tennis regularly, and represent both my local club and Ulster. I taught PE for 35 years and was head of department in a local secondary school. I coached my school teams, took area netball squads and ran courses, and started a local club which I coached at junior and senior level for 10 years. I am an active netball umpire.

Netball is still a huge part of my life and I get great pleasure from seeing players, including my daughter and two granddaughters, getting involved and benefitting from this great game. I thank netball too for lifelong friends and great socialising. My heartfelt thanks to all those wonderful, influential people who helped me along the way.

ACHIEVEMENTS

Played in 5 World Netball Championships

More than 100 netball caps for Northern Ireland

Played for Northern Ireland in Home International Championships

Helped NI achieve highest-ever world ranking: 7th (1983) equalled in 2018

SUSIE RODGERS MBE

PARALYMPIC SWIMMING

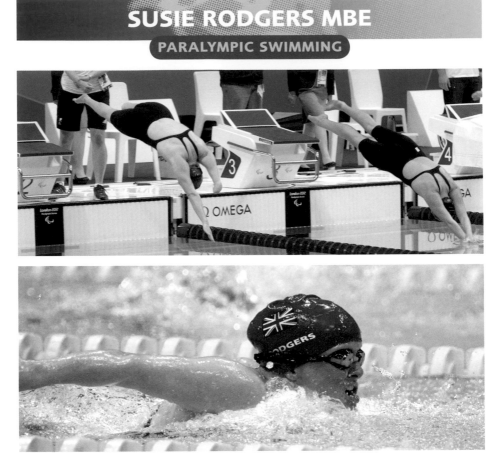

How I first became involved in sport

I became involved in sport quite late in life. I didn't really come across opportunities when I was younger, as Paralympic sport did not have the profile that it has today. However, I always tried to take part in any physical activity when I was young but very often competed against able-bodied athletes, and naturally assumed that I was not as good. I only got involved as I started work and trained around my full-time job for several years until I started to break into the national scene. Once I was selected for my first international competition (European championships, Berlin 2011), I stayed on the team until retirement, but kept my professional work going on a part-time basis at the same time.

ACHIEVEMENTS

Paralympic Games gold medal, 50m butterfly (Rio 2016)

Paralympic Games bronze medals, 50m freestyle & 400m freestyle (Rio 2016)

Paralympic Games bronze medals, (100m freestyle, 400m freestyle and 4 x 100m freestyle relay (London 2012)

During a six-year career as an athlete won 30 international medals at World & European level & have been European, World & Paralympic champion

Retired from elite sport in 2017 as undefeated European champion & a multiple British & European record holder

Appointed MBE in 2017

Inspiration

I was inspired watching the Paralympic Games in Beijing in 2008 on TV and seeing people representing their country whom I had met in competitions when I was still at university. I was impressed by the standard and I loved watching it all. I knew London 2012 was around the corner. I was working in London at the time, so I thought it would be wonderful to aim for a home Games, basing all my training in the city where I was living and working. It was a fantastic time in my life.

Memories

When I won gold in Rio in 2016, I was so shocked I reacted with an open-mouthed look of disbelief – so much so that it became a shock face which trended with an emoji on Twitter! It was a genuine reaction. I always wanted to win, but knew it would be so hard to do. Yet, I managed to get there and it was a lovely moment for me.

What I am doing now

I am currently working at the BPA (British Paralympic Association) and learning about the sport from the inside. I sit on several boards externally and enjoy being a non-executive director. I see myself continuing an international career – my passion is languages and different cultures – and hope to continue in that area for years to come.

FREYA ROSS (NÉE MURRAY)

How I first became involved in sport

When I was young, I tried lots of different activities – gymnastics, badminton, swimming, skiing, climbing and, of course, running. At first it was just for fun, but as I have got older I have realized there are so many other benefits too.

Inspiration

My older brother and sister encouraged me to take up athletics, and most of the other sports I tried. Whenever they did something, I wanted to be involved too. I recall thinking, when my brother competed for the Scottish Schools Cross-Country that I'd like to represent my country too. I also looked up to other Scottish athletes – Yvonne Murray and Liz McColgan – when I was very young, and to Kelly Holmes and Paula Radcliffe when I was a bit older.

Memories

Some years ago, I went away for a weekend in Berlin with friends. On the morning that we were due to leave I got up early so that I would have time to go for a run before heading off. Unfortunately, I hadn't altered the time on my alarm clock so I got up an hour later than I thought. When I got back from my run, my friends were all standing outside the place where we were staying, looking agitated and shouting, 'We need to go, NOW.' I tried to look cool, as I couldn't understand why they were so concerned ... there was plenty of time to catch our flight. When they told me the real time, it dawned on me what I had done. We had to run to the nearest taxi rank, with me still in my athletics gear, and dash to the airport. We made it, just ... but they never let me forget what I nearly cost them.

ACHIEVEMENTS
Olympic Games marathon, 44th (London 2012)
Commonwealth Games, 10,000m (5th) &
5,000m (7th) (Delhi 2010)

ANN SARGENT (NÉE WILSON)

Inspiration

I happened to have the flu during the 1964 Olympic Games in Tokyo, which I suppose was quite fortunate. I remember watching the 800m and Ann Packer coming from the back to win, with David Colman (BBC) commentating. Although this was not my event, I decided there and then I wanted to go the next Olympics in Mexico, and I did. I recall my international debut for England in a Home Nations meeting in 1965, when I first went up against Mary Peters. I beat her in the high jump and the long jump, but she got very much better after that!

How I first became involved in sport

At junior school I found I was so much better than everyone else – even the boys and my teacher, Mr Shorney, encouraged me to join an athletics club. Happily, the running track was only about 100m from my house. I really loved it and never missed training, even though it meant sometimes not being able to go out socially with my friends. I was coached by George Holroyd and started mainly with high jump. I did that for a little while but George was a good coach and would get us to do other events, which was good. I had a go at the high hurdles and did well and that's where my multi-eventing started.

Memories

I remember being on the blocks at the start of my hurdles race at the Munich Olympics in 1972, and my hands literally trembling. I've always thought 'experience' is over-rated. The more you know, the worse it is. It's better to be young and unafraid. Perhaps I could have trained harder in my athletics career, but I had a job in a bank and had to balance training with working, which was hard.

I used to come home from work and then go to train – I'd have to hop over the fence if the track at Southchurch Park in Southend (Essex) was closed, which it was every day apart from Tuesdays, Thursdays and Sunday mornings. The floodlights wouldn't be on at the track so ⇒

I'd have to train using the streetlights for illumination, and it was always a cinder track rather than tartan/all weather.

Under the circumstances, I felt I performed reasonably well. I am slightly envious of the modern-day athletes who have their own trainers and lots of support. People have always asked about my rivalry with Mary (Peters) but it was never a problem for me. I thought we got on very well and respect her achievements enormously.

GOLDIE SAYERS

How I first become involved in sport

I started by playing sport with my brother in the back garden. He was three years older than me and laid back, whereas I was very competitive and wanted to beat him at everything. When I got to school, my favourite time of the week was when we played against other schools. I was a team sport player predominantly but could always throw a ball a long way. My PE teacher asked if I would compete for the school in the javelin in the summer term. I was actually given a javelin to take home over the Easter holiday, to 'try out'! That wouldn't happen now because of Health & Safety concerns, but I'm very glad that I did. Although I didn't know it at the time, I was being offered the chance of a career in sport. I practised for hours in the garden trying to get this awkward thing to fly. When I had outgrown the garden, I would cycle around my local area trying to find a bigger field in which to practise. I took my javelin back to school and was entered for the County Schools' competition, which I won, but more importantly was introduced to my first coach. Within a month I had improved 10m and went on to win the English Schools title. Just eight years later I was walking

out into a 60,000-seater stadium at my first Olympic Games, in Athens, 2004.

Inspiration

The Olympic Games were my inspiration. I was 10 when I watched the Barcelona Games, and from that moment I really wanted to compete for my country at sport. One of the most inspiring races I have ever seen was when the Australian, Cathy Freeman won the 400m in Sydney 2000, with the weight of a nation on her shoulders. It was very similar for Jess Ennis-Hill in London 2012. Both athletes handled the pressure and expectation with great grace.

Memories

I fell flat on my face during the run-up in my first junior international in Alicante. Fortunately, it was in the warm-up but it was still very embarrassing for a 15 year-old who was looking to impress.

ACHIEVEMENTS

Olympic Games bronze medal, javelin (Beijing 2008)

Olympic Games Team GB (Athens 2004, Beijing 2008 & London 2012)

European Cup of Winter Throwing gold medal, javelin (Split 2008)

11 times National champion

British Athletics team captain, 2014

British record, 2007, 2008 & 2012

First British woman to throw over 65m since javelins were redesigned in 1999

ATHLETICS
DIANE SEAMAN (NÉE COATES)

How I first became involved in sport

I remember acquiring a fondness for throwing things, by chucking snowballs at lads coming home from school. Later, I recall almost spearing an official with my javelin at an athletics club meeting

Memories

While Chris Chataway was running a race at the White City in the 1950s, I looked after his younger brother for him. When we were given our international vests, we had to sew on our own badges. I also sewed on Roger Bannister's for him.

ACHIEVEMENTS
Olympic Games finalist, Javelin (Helsinki 1952)
Former British record holder, Javelin (1952)

ATHLETICS

WENDY SLY MBE (NÉE SMITH)

How I first became involved in sport

I loved every sport at school including netball, football and running and I was also a keen swimmer. My PE teacher suggested that I join the local athletics club as I was quite a quick runner. My parents could only afford one sport and I chose athletics. I joined the junior group in February 1971, aged 11. Cross-country was happening and I got involved in that too. I started finishing quite high

up in races – there is nothing like a bit of success to inspire you to train harder! Success then followed on the track, and the rest is history.

Inspiration

Lillian Board was a great inspiration and showed what a woman could do in what was then the longest event for female runners (800m). For a skinny, plain teenager from Feltham, she was an icon of glamour and guts, at a distance I also ran myself, and a very brave woman in the face of adversity.

Memories

I wore red socks for a while thinking I would then be able to run like David Bedford. He was everyone's hero in the Seventies. I even queued for his autograph once, never knowing he would one day be a friend. 🔥

ACHIEVEMENTS

Olympic Games silver medal, 3,000m (Los Angeles 1984)

Olympic Games 7th 3,000m (Seoul 1988)

World Road Race Championships, gold medal, 10,000m (San Diego 1983)

Commonwealth Games silver medal, 3,000m (Brisbane 1982)

Appointed MBE in 2015

ATHLETICS

ATHLETICS
JANET SMITH

How I first became involved in sport

I have always loved sport and especially athletics right from when I was at junior school. PE was always my favourite lesson of the week. The junior school was lucky to have a swimming pool in the grounds but I hated swimming! It was always athletics I loved.

Inspiration

I have always loved the Olympic Games and remember watching Olga Korbut in the 1972 Games from Munich. Daley Thompson and Torvill and Dean were also big inspirations for me.

Memories

I remember well, the first time I threw over 50m in the hammer. I was at a competition in Belgium. In those days, that was the bench mark of being a UK top 10 athlete.

One of my earliest memories is of a ballet exam when I was much younger. The certificate mentioned: 'Janet must learn to keep her tongue in whilst dancing.' This trait has never left me and most photos I see of me hammer throwing, my tongue is out. It's all subconscious!

What I am doing now

I am very fortunate to be able to work in a field I love and have been with the British Olympic Association for over 15 years. When I was at school, my project for my history exam was on the Olympic Games. I never dreamt that 25 years later I would be working for them.

I still regularly compete in athletics for both my club and then in Masters competitions in the UK and abroad. I also am a qualified field official which is my way of giving back to the sport I love.

ACHIEVEMENTS

I have been throwing the hammer for 27 years now and my greatest achievement came in 2013 when I won the World Masters Championships in Brazil competing in the weight throw (Heavy Hammer). The age range group that I compete with is a very strong one so winning any global medal is an achievement, which I am pleased to have done a few times since 2001.

ATHLETICS

JOYCE SMITH MBE

How I first became involved in sport

I had some success at school, winning the long jump at the Hertfordshire Schools Championships, but the farthest we were allowed to run was 150yds. We went to a holiday camp one summer and I won some sprint races, so I decided to go to a local athletics club in 1954 to try the sport seriously and make new friends. When I was asked to run 880yds in a trophy meeting to collect points for the club team, I won in a record time and that inspired me to stay in the sport and at longer distances. I couldn't make the club team as sprinter.

Memories

When my granddaughter Lauren was at secondary school, one of her IT lessons was an introduction to the internet. The teacher explained that the net was an excellent opportunity to find out things you don't know about. He added: 'For example, I don't suppose any of you know who won the first London Marathon.'

Lauren put her hand up and said: 'I know, it was my granny.'

The teacher replied: 'Very funny Lauren, now let's be sensible.'

Lauren insisted: 'But she did!'

The teacher enquired: 'And who is your granny?'

Lauren replied: 'Joyce Smith.'

The teacher replied: 'Oh. Now you'll have to look up something different ...'

Another pupil spoke up suggesting an apology was in order, which Lauren did receive.

ACHIEVEMENTS

Olympic Games semi-finalist, 1500m (Munich 1972)

European Championships bronze medal, 3,000m (Rome 1974)

Tokyo Marathon Winner (1979 & 1980)

London Marathon Winner (1981 & 1982)

IAAF World Cross-Country Championships gold medal (Cambridge 1972), silver medal (Waregem 1973) & bronze medal (San Sebastian 1971)

Appointed MBE in 1984

ATHLETICS

KELLY SOTHERTON

How I first became involved in sport

I was good at sport at school from a very young age, and naturally competitive. I was always winning on sports days and beating the boys. My mum was never pushy and allowed me to do whatever I wanted, so I played netball and hockey up to 16 and carried on netball into university, as well as athletics. I used to bring a football to school so I guess the enthusiasm was just in me.

Inspiration

I didn't have a sporting hero on my wall as a kid. I was never in to watch TV as I was always out playing sport or getting into mischief. I worked from the age of 14 so had limited telly time. I was particularly lucky in having great PE teachers who were encouraging at all times. Mr Smith at my middle school encouraged me to join an athletics club on the mainland as I am from the Isle of Wight, where facilities were very limited.

Memories

During the Athens Olympics in 2004, I received a little hand-written note from Mary (Peters) to say how happy she was to see me win a medal. Also, I shared an apartment with Kelly Holmes among others and she was the only one up waiting for me when I got back from the track with my own medal. Kelly had said she wished she had had someone waiting for her when she had won her first Olympic medal in Sydney. She had her 800m final less than 48 hours later so for her to be up at 1am waiting for me was amazing. Obviously, I feel I helped her win her gold!

What I am doing today

I am part of the IAAF Woman's Committee and set up an athlete sub-group for UKA anti-doping PST. I am a board member for Sports People Think Tank (real issues in sports which are raised by sports people and researched by academics who then make recommendations which are passed to relevant authorities). I am also a NED Board member, on Adullam Housing Association, a mentor for British Weightlifting and a mentor on AASE program for UKA. I also do talks, and appearances and some media.

ACHIEVEMENTS

Olympic Games bronze medal, heptathlon (Athens 2004)

Olympic Games bronze medal, heptathlon & 4 x 400m relay (Beijing 2008)

World Championships bronze medal, heptathlon (Osaka 2007)

World Indoor Championships silver medal, pentathlon (Valencia 2008)

European Indoor Championships silver medal, pentathlon (Madrid 2005 & Birmingham 2007) 4 x 400m relay (Paris 2011)

Commonwealth Games gold medal, heptathlon (Melbourne 2006)

GOLF

VICKI THOMAS

How I first became involved in sport

My mother and father were both keen golfers so all three of us (children) followed in their footsteps. My father coached me from the age of 12 until I was 16 or 17, by which time I had been selected for my county (Glamorgan) and for international duties. I continued to play for Wales from that early age, and even until this day still play for Wales at senior level.

Inspiration

In that time I was very fortunate not to receive any injuries or setbacks, and was coached by many extremely good coaches, especially Maureen Madill at Portstewart.

> "... the first time that a British golf team, amateur or professional, had won on USA soil."

Memories

Winning the Curtis Cup in 1986 at Kansas City was the first time that Great Britain & Ireland had regained the cup since 1956, and also the first time that a British golf team, amateur or professional, had won on USA soil.

ACHIEVEMENTS

Individual
Glamorgan County champion
Welsh stroke/match play champion
British stroke play champion

Team
GB Commonwealth team (1979, 1983, 1987, 1991)
GB & Ireland Curtis Cup team (1982, 1984, 1986, 1988, 1990, 1992)
Glamorgan County team (1970–2008)
Carmarthen & Pembrokeshire team (2009–2014)
Welsh junior team (1969–1973)
Welsh senior team (2005–2014)

ICE DANCING

JAYNE TORVILL OBE

How I first became involved in sport

I went on a school trip to my local skating rink in Nottingham at the age of eight and immediately fell in love with it. I was very lucky to have the opportunity to take it further as my parents drove me to practice every weekend. After a year I finally got my own boots and skates.

Inspiration

When I first started skating seriously with Christopher in 1975, I was inspired by Russian skaters. They were particularly dominant at that time, and they made me appreciate the level that would be required to be a champion performer.

Memories

When we were on tour with our *Dancing On Ice* show, we were skating on a small rink. It had a tiny perimeter and the edge of the rink was only 2ft high. I was up on Christopher's back for part of the routine, facing the edge, when he got a bit confused and we hit it. I managed to jump clear but he fell right over it. It was meant to be a serious piece but once I established that he was OK, we just couldn't stop laughing.

I have known Mary for many years and I recall going on a cruise with her in around 2000, together with Sharron Davies and Lynn Davies. We always sat for meals together, giggling and laughing at various recollections, and having drinks together in a cabin afterwards. It was such an enjoyable time. Mary P and I also competed together on the BBC TV quiz show *Pointless Celebrities*, which we hoped didn't refer to us!

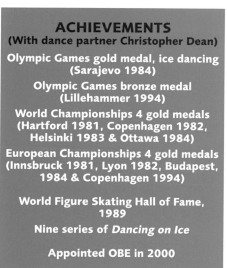

ACHIEVEMENTS
(With dance partner Christopher Dean)

Olympic Games gold medal, ice dancing (Sarajevo 1984)

Olympic Games bronze medal (Lillehammer 1994)

World Championships 4 gold medals (Hartford 1981, Copenhagen 1982, Helsinki 1983 & Ottawa 1984)

European Championships 4 gold medals (Innsbruck 1981, Lyon 1982, Budapest, 1984 & Copenhagen 1994)

World Figure Skating Hall of Fame, 1989

Nine series of *Dancing on Ice*

Appointed OBE in 2000

What I am doing now

I have done pantomime, which was not only good fun but very hard work. We were the Fairy Godparents in Cinderella. It was on roller blades rather than ice and it was certainly a challenge. We were on the stage for the whole production and there was also a lot of dialogue, which doesn't usually feature in our ice dance routines!

TENNIS

CHRISTINE TRUMAN MBE

How I first became involved in sport

After the war my parents, who met at a tennis club in Leytonstone, were given a net to put up in the garden, so that my four older brothers and sisters could try to play tennis. I was the fifth of six children and my only ambition at the age of eight or nine was to be good enough to join in the family foursome. However, I was constantly told I wasn't good enough and could only be a ball girl!! They did eventually become ideal practice partners, but trying to keep up with them is how I started.

Inspiration

There were two: Maureen Connolly, usually known as Little Mo, and Lottie Dod, who won Wimbledon at the age of 15 in 1887. Maureen had won all the Grand Slams by the age of 19 and I wanted to beat both their records. That's why my best results were when I was young. I never equalled their records, but they inspired me to try to be good at a young age.

Memories

As runner-up at Wimbledon in 1961, I was given a voucher for just £15 and £10 for each of my semi-finals. For winning the French, Italian & Swiss, I won £40 to help cover the trip. This was a different era! My kit was made by the fashion designer Teddy Tingling, and my rackets and shoes were supplied by Slazenger. Travel was by invitation only. All very different when compared to today's tennis millionaires.

ACHIEVEMENTS
Grand Slam singles
French W (1959)
Australian W (1960)
Wimbledon F (1961)
US F (1959)
Grand Slam doubles
Australia W (1960)

**Italian & Swiss singles champion
(both 1959)**

Appointed MBE in 2001

BETH TWEDDLE MBE

achieve amazing results. When I first started gymnastics I wasn't a big fan of it. I used to do anything to get out of going and actually gave up soon after I first started, before a coach in my first gym club encouraged me to come back and join in. It was only when I did my first competition, when I was eight, that I realized it was really what I wanted to do.

Memories

One of my most embarrassing memories was when I forgot my floor routine. It was in 2006, when I was 21, and I had to adapt the routine and change it just before I competed because the floor wasn't too good. Halfway through, I realized I had gone into autopilot and done the normal version of my routine and was way ahead of time and had to improvise. I decided then that I was definitely not going to become a choreographer any time soon. 🎗

How I first became involved in sport

Sport has played a big part in my life since I was born. I grew up with a hockey stick in my hand but it wasn't for me. I tried a lot of other sports and then eventually found gymnastics when I was seven. My parents knew that sport was for me as I was very hyperactive as a child and could never sit still!

Inspiration

As I got older, Kelly Holmes and Paula Radcliffe both had an impact as, like me, they had injuries but also managed to

ACHIEVEMENTS

Olympic Games bronze medal, (London 2012)

World Cup gold medals (2007, 2009, 2010, 2012)

European Championships gold medals (2009, 2010, 2011) & silver (2008)

Appointed MBE in 2010

ROWING
PENELOPE VINCENT-SWEET

How I first became involved in sport

My parents always encouraged me to do a sport that I enjoyed. I loved swimming and joined a club, and after a few years moved on to springboard diving. At school I was hopeless at any game involving balls, but enjoyed the swimming and trampolining.

Inspiration

My father used to take me along to Eights Week in Oxford, where we had to shout for the 3rd Exeter team (which had been 'his' boat). I was fascinated by the rowing, which seemed so sophisticated compared to the canoeing I'd done with the Girl Guides. As soon as I got to Cambridge I enrolled in the college boat club and never looked back!

My coaches and my teammates all inspired me to train hard, give the best of myself and try to win each race. It was always for something greater than myself: my college, my university and my country. There was always the dream of a gold medal.

I don't remember being particularly aware of sports personalities, but I do remember Mary Peters gaining her Olympic gold medal in 1972.

ACHIEVEMENTS

Olympic Games finalist, fifth in eights (Moscow 1980)

Boat Race, rowed in winning crew for Cambridge University vs Oxford (1979)

Stroked the Clare College May IV to Head of the River (1979)

Memories

There was a 'skirt incident,' which occurred in the run-up to the Moscow Olympics, when our official outfits were made-to-measure. We were invited afterwards to a posh London Club for lunch, so wore our new outfits immediately. Our host, who had laid on a generous buffet, was puzzled why we all stayed standing rather than sitting in the comfortable chairs provided. The explanation: whether from pure bad design or from a desire to cut costs our wraparound skirts had so little overlap that if we sat down they opened to a quite indecent degree. When he discovered this, he fetched a pile of enormous table napkins which we could spread over our laps when we sat down to eat!

Once in Moscow, I recall a session about how to reduce our wind resistance. We came up with the idea of borrowing swimming caps but backed out, afraid that our coach would take it badly.

More than 20 years after my Olympic experience, I saw a TV programme about an East German athlete who'd been in the same Olympics as me, and was now suing her government for having given her performance-enhancing drugs and ruining her health. It brought home to me how lucky I was. Even though I had no Olympic medal, I had my good health and three thriving children.

ATHLETICS
FATIMA WHITBREAD MBE

How I first became involved in sport

I spent the first 14 years of my life in children's homes having been abandoned as a baby, although some might say 'left to die'. A neighbour heard me crying in a flat in London but saw no one going in or out for three days. She reported it to the police who came and knocked down the door and rescued me. I was taken into hospital where I spent four months recovering from malnutrition and a rash infection. Sport was my saviour as a youngster, indeed it kept me out of trouble and focused. Because of my circumstances, I had been an emotionally troubled little girl, not knowing what love and security felt like – which most children should have as a birthright. I learned very quickly that sport earned me respect from my peers and gave me self-worth and confidence, something I didn't get from being in a children's home, and I realized quickly that this was where my future lay.

Inspiration

There was a very special moment during my life in the children's home that was instrumental in my desire to become an Olympian. I was just 11 when I saw Mary Peters winning a gold medal in the pentathlon at the 1972 Olympics in Munich. She inspired me greatly with her ⇒

humble beginnings – a girl from Northern Ireland, made good. Unknown to me at the time, of course, Mary would become my Team Manager for the Los Angeles Olympics and many World, European and International events in the 1980s.

Memories

The press wrote an article where Margaret Thatcher and I were photographed together, with the caption: 'Britain's two strongest women'. No need to explain that one! However, I must add that I was very fortunate to find the love of the Whitbread family at the age of 14. Together with the grit and determination I learned in the children's home and growing up as a 'tough nut to crack', I won 11 major medals in different World, European and Commonwealth events in a career that spanned 20 years. My circumstances certainly inspired me too.

What I am doing now

I still enjoy my fitness to this day, and my son Ryan Norman is also very sporty. Sport today is a way of life and should be enjoyed by everyone.

ACHIEVEMENTS

Olympic Games bronze medal, javelin
(Los Angeles 1984)

Olympic Games silver medal, javelin
(Seoul 1988)

World Championships silver medal
(Helsinki 1983)

World Championships gold medal
(Rome 1987)

European Championships gold medal
(Stuttgart 1986)

Commonwealth Games bronze medal
(Brisbane 1982)

Commonwealth Games silver medal
(Edinburgh 1986)

Appointed MBE in 1988
BBC Sports Personality of the Year 1987

ATHLETICS

STEFFI WILSON

How I first became involved in sport

My mum was an international hockey player, and she always encouraged me to participate in everything I could.

Inspiration

My mum came with me everywhere when I competed in sport, and she was my shoulder to cry on. She was always that right balance between encouraging and empathetic. She was always finding solutions as to how I could improve, and she made a lot of sacrifices to come and support me, whatever I wanted to do.

Memories

In my first season of athletics, my aim was to run at the English Schools' Athletics Championships, for which you have to run under a certain time to qualify. The first time I ran that time, in the 200m, my mum had brought me new shorts to try, which were a little bit baggier than normal. Halfway round the bend, I could feel them starting to fall. I was so terrified, I ran the rest of the race holding my shorts up, yet ran a new personal best and achieved the English Schools' standard.

ACHIEVEMENTS

European Junior gold medal, 4 x 100m relay (2013)

National Indoor U20 silver medal, 60m (Birmingham 2012)

National Outdoor U20 bronze medal, 100m (Bedford 2015)

169

MOTOR RACING

SUSIE WOLFF MBE

How I first became involved in sport

My father owned a motorbike shop in Scotland and had a real passion for both bikes and racing them, so it was inevitable that something of it would rub off on me. We were generally very sporty – we liked skiing too – and it was one of the beauties of having a family interest that we could enjoy things together.

I wasn't any good at ball sports at school, which were dominated by the boys, so I was open to trying something else in which I could possibly excel. When I was just eight I got involved with karting. I had always enjoyed the adrenalin rush of going fast on skis, and quickly developed a similar feeling in a kart. While dad was off racing on his bike, my brother and I would play on the go-karts. It became a passion.

Inspiration

My parents' support was crucial. They not only put me in the position of being able to 'have a go' but also made it clear that it was up to me whether or not I carried on with any form of sport, and competed. There was no pressure from them, which was great.

When I did switch up a gear, so to speak, into Formula Renault and Formula Three there was really no other woman driver at that level to look up to, so I always had a sense of being the first in that regard. However, as a Scot, I did always enjoy seeing David Coulthard do well in Formula One races.

Once I started making progress in motorsport, I was on my own ... and therefore a self-motivator. I was competing in a world full of men and it was tough. No one wanted to be beaten by a woman, least of all teammates, and they made that clear. That was inspiration in itself for me to do a fantastic job.

Memories

In Germany, my sponsors made me drive a pink car, which inevitably, got a lot of coverage. If I'm honest, I hated it. It was such a cliché ... the blonde driver in the pink Mercedes. It was another possible reason for people not to take me seriously. I drove the car, of course, but it made me a target and a tough job became even harder.

What I am doing now

When I announced my retirement three years ago, it was my choice to do so. The time was right and I have no regrets. My husband Toto (executive director of the Mercedes Formula One team) and I have a son (Jack). I hope I can be an inspiration to other women in motor racing and help them make progress in the sport.

ACHIEVEMENTS

British Grand Prix (Silverstone 2014) in a Williams. First woman in 22 years to take part in a Formula One race weekend

British Woman Kart Racing Driver of the Year (1996 &1997)

Formula Renault driver (2001–2004)

Formula Renault UK Championship, 5th overall (with 3 podium finishes) (2004)

Formula Three driver (2005)

DTM German Touring Car Series driver (2006–2012)

Williams Formula One development driver (2012–2014) test driver (2015)

Ambassador for Mercedes (since 2016)

Principal, Venturi Formula E team (2018)

Appointed MBE in 2017

ISABEL WOODS
LONG-DISTANCE CYCLING

How I first became involved in sport

I was born in 1928, just prior to the years of the Depression. I didn't have a bicycle as a child due to the extreme poverty at that time. Later, my parents were reluctant to buy me one as I had inherited my father's short-sightedness. I started working in a timber firm at the age of 16, and it took me another two years to save enough money to buy my first bike. We were living in Belfast, and the bicycle enabled me to escape the city. Both my parents came from farming backgrounds, which probably explains my great love of the countryside and my drive to find a way of accessing it. Shortly afterwards, my sister Nan acquired her first bike (at the age of 20) and together we enjoyed the pleasures of touring and hostelling.

Inspiration

We kept fit in the winter by joining the Trinity Harriers Club where we met Ena McKeown, a very enthusiastic cyclist who was well-known in ladies' racing circles and had been since the mid-1930s. She was canvassing for recruits to enter the Ulster Ladies Road Club novice five-mile time trial (this was in 1949) and we agreed to take part. I was second fastest and was encouraged to try again by the club members. I joined the ULRC and competed successfully in all their trials that season. I also bought a new racing bike! In 1949, I was approached by Bobby McGregor, the highly-respected trainer of Glentoran Football Club, and I agreed to allow him to advise me about training. The following season, I competed in all the club races, set new records and won the best all-rounder cup, thanks in part to his guidance and encouragement.

Memories

In 1953, I accompanied Ena on a cycle tour to the South of France. We agreed that, on our return, we would attempt some of the long distance place-to-place records for which the Belfast Cycling Club was renowned. Ena chose the Derry-to-Belfast, I did the Enniskillen-to-Belfast and so began my succession of long-distance endeavours.

I recall attempting my Ireland 'end-to-end record' from Mizen Head to Fair Head. There was a long climb out of Cork called Water Glass Hill, which I reached at dusk, and suddenly became aware of the vast journey ahead of me. Suddenly, out of the gloom, a shower of flower petals were strewn in my path – a truly continental gesture, which gave me a great boost just when I needed it. The people responsible were the McCarthy family from Cork. Carl was a well-known, outstanding cyclist who

ACHIEVEMENTS

Irish record-holder for Belfast-Dublin, Belfast-Dublin-Belfast, Mizen Head-Fair Head & Dublin-Derry distance riding (all set in the 1950s)

Northern Ireland record-holder for Belfast–Enniskillen, Belfast–Enniskillen-Belfast, 100-mile time trial & 24hr distance trial

Numerous national championship titles & time trial victories

would have been very familiar with this part of the course, and would have known the sections where a little encouragement might be appreciated. It certainly was. Even 60 years later, this is one of my most treasured memories.

173

ATHLETICS

PIPPA WOOLVEN

How I first became involved in sport

Coming from a very sporty family, my involvement in athletics was almost inevitable. My parents were very encouraging when it came to my participating in as many sports as possible from an early age and fortunately there were plenty of opportunities to do so. I joined my local athletics club (Wycombe Phoenix Harriers) at age 13 with a couple of friends and never looked back. My main motivation to go to training to begin with was for the water fights we would have at the end of a session on a hot summer's day, but soon I got hooked on the sport itself and I don't think there's been a day when I haven't thought about running since.

Inspiration

My three older siblings were a big source of inspiration growing up. All of them played sports at an international level and my competitive nature drove me to try and be as successful as they were.

I also looked up to several sporting icons such as Muhammad Ali (I loved his quotes and unbelievably strong belief in himself) and Paula Radcliffe, who taught me that ordinary people could achieve extraordinary things.

Memories

One of my coolest sporting experiences was when Usain Bolt spotted me trying to take a picture of him on my phone in the warm-up area before my race at the Commonwealth Games. He walked over to me laughing before taking a photo of *me* on his friend's camera to embarrass me. That definitely helped get my pulse rate going before the race! 🔥

ACHIEVEMENTS

Commonwealth Games finalist, 3,000m steeplechase (Glasgow 2014)

British Universities & Colleges Athletics Championships gold medal, 2,000m steeplechase (London 2012).
First gold medal awarded in the new Olympic stadium

World Junior Championships 3,000m steeplechase (Barcelona 2012)

MARTINE WRIGHT MBE

PARALYMPIC SITTING VOLLEYBALL

How I first became involved in sport

As a survivor of the London terrorist bombings in 2005, the day after London was chosen as hosts for the 2012 Olympic and Paralympic Games, I was looking for something to help me rebuild my life after such a trauma. I couldn't go back to work at my old job, I wasn't brave enough to compare the old Martine with the new one without my legs. I was searching for something to rekindle my old drive and ambition. My dear physio, Maggie, suggested I try sport. Stoke Mandeville hospital was hosting a day for people with a disability to try out different sports. I tried archery – OK, but no; tennis – pretty good; fencing – definitely not. Then there was sitting volleyball, the only sport I could play OUT of my wheelchair. I loved it from the word go. Little did I know then but it would heal me: not just get me fit physically, but mentally and psychologically. I loved the team dynamic and the laughs and being with women who had all understood the nature of trauma. Most importantly, it gave me the chance to dream again. It made me believe that I had always been meant to do this 'journey' from near death to the greatest day of my life at the Excel Arena, with my family, including my little son, sitting in the crowd crying with happiness.

Inspiration

My biggest inspiration was my mum, who held my face in her hands, looked me in the eyes and instilled in me the belief that my life could still have meaning even though I'd lost my legs. 'You're still Martine!' she said. Then, of course, there was my lovely husband, my son, my dad, my brother and sister, my wider family, my friends, the NHS and my wonderful physio Maggie. I realize now that it was as much for them as me that I was bursting with pride when I sat on that volleyball court for the first time at the Paralympics, in 2012. It was my way of saying: 'You see, after all the desperate times we've been through, life's not so bad, is it? In fact, we're happy and we're achieving together things that I would never have dreamed possible.' I'll never forget that moment. I have it captured forever on a framed picture on our wall at home. My son, Oscar, sitting on his dad's shoulders in the arena, holding up a sign saying: 'Go mummy Go!' and family and friends sitting all around with my mum and their tears of happiness.

Memories

As I looked at the crowd that day, I could barely see my dad behind a HUGE banner that he was waving in my honour. 'Where on earth could he have got that from?' I wondered fleetingly. All was revealed in due course. In the excitement of the match, he accidentally reversed the banner at some point revealing the words on the other side: *Slimming World! Sign up today. First Week Free*. He'd 'borrowed' the banner from the local British Legion club so that he'd have something to wave.

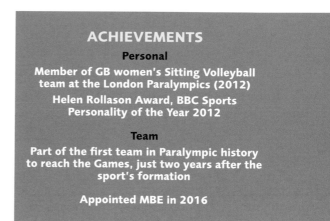

ACHIEVEMENTS

Personal

Member of GB women's Sitting Volleyball team at the London Paralympics (2012)

Helen Rollason Award, BBC Sports Personality of the Year 2012

Team

Part of the first team in Paralympic history to reach the Games, just two years after the sport's formation

Appointed MBE in 2016

What I am doing now

I'm still involved with the GB Women's Sitting Volleyball team, luckily for me. It's a sport where at least one player in Slovenia is still going at the age of 76, so there's no rush for me to retire. I am an inspirational speaker, which is something I love. I am also an ambassador for a number of charities, and a hospital volunteer, involved in mentoring or just speaking to patients who may have been through some kind of traumatic incident. I'm a wife and mum too, a daughter, a sister and a friend. So, life gets very hectic, especially when you factor in Daisy the dog too!

I'm an author as well, now. I was very proud when my book *Unbroken* was published in 2017. It was a reminder of how much I'd been through and the amazing, loving people who helped me not just survive but become happier than I had ever been before. That's my message really. You can overcome anything with belief, and the support of amazing people around you.

ROWING

FRANCESCA ZINO

How I first became involved in sport

Growing up, I was always involved in some form of running activity in the playground, be it such varied games as British Bulldogs, tennis, etc. At secondary school, sport played a key part of my experience, being in the tennis teams, lacrosse teams and heading up my house as Sports Captain.

Inspiration

At university, rowing was a way to socialise and meet people while doing something I enjoyed and made me feel good. It was also a good way to relieve stress at times. Luckily our novice rowing crew was highly successful which inspired me to take the first steps to taking up the sport really seriously. This culminated in me getting to the Olympic Games in Sydney 2000, representing GB in the Women's 8+.

Memories

After Sydney I retired from the team and had no clear direction on what career I would pursue. However, sport was always the constant means of making me feel good more often than not – be it amateur tennis knockabouts in Battersea Park or running the London Marathon. I decided I needed a challenge after giving up rowing, and I did it, despite having always hated running. I ran the course in four hours and love it now. I also took on the challenge of the London Triathlon for a couple of years.

What I am doing now

I'm living in Hong Kong, where I did row for the first three years I was here. I now do outrigger canoe on the sea for the Royal Hong Kong Yacht Club. We've participated in races locally but also in Singapore and Guam, and in other races in Hawaii. It continues to be a staple of my daily life, and something which my social life has revolved around. I also trail-run here and dragon boat. I am a sucker for sport it would seem but equally enjoy 'down days' when I don't do anything at all.

ACHIEVEMENTS

Olympics Games GB team member, W8+ (Sydney 2000)
World Championships U23 gold medal, W2 (Milan 1997)
World Championships bronze medal, W8+ (Aiguebelette 1997)
Cambridge University Blue Boat (1997)

ACKNOWLEDGEMENTS

PICTURE CREDITS

Alamy –
Cover: (Jessica Ennis-Hill, Christina Ohuruogu,
Tanni Grey-Tompson),
pp 3, 4, 7 (both), 8–9, 11 (both), 12, 13, 14, 15, 21, 22,
23, 24–25, 27, 29, 34, 36, 40–41, 52, 53, 61, 67, 68, 69,
75, 77, 80–81, 82, 84, 94, 98, 99, 102, 106, 122, 123,
124, 125, 141, 144, 145, 150 (both), 155 (base), 162,
163, 165, 169, 170, 171, 172, 174, 176

Athletes' own –
Cover: (Mary Peters),
p10 (base), pp 17, 18–19, 26, 33, 42, 43, 44, 45, 50, 51,
54, 56, 62, 64–65, 70, 72, 73, 86, 87, 88, 89, 90, 94, 96,
100, 104, 107, 112(right), 119, 120, 121, 125(right),
126, 128, 129, 131, 140, 142, 148, 149, 156, 157, 158,
159, 165 (base), 167, 173, 175

Ghetty – pp 59, 78, 112(left), 160
Ian MacNicol, cover and p60
Mark Pritchard, cover
Press Association, p2, 119

SkyUK/ Andrea Southam, p10 (top)
Mark Shearman, p10 (base)
Jonathan Faulds, p35
Scott Chalmers, pp37, 38
Michael Loveder, p46
David Hartley, p75 (base)
Chris Andrews, p94
Mark Doherty, pp114, 115
Tom Russell, p120 (both)
Hope Photography p121
Photorun, p140
Sports Sphere, p155 (top)

Images have been received from a number of sources including the
picture libraries and photographers credited. A number have come
direct from the participants or their governing bodies and every
effort has been made to check and trace the copyright holders.
In the event of any errors or omissions please contact the
publisher who will rectify the matter in subsequent editions

PUBLISHED BY
Gateway Publishing Ltd
www.gatewaysark.co.uk

A catalogue record for this book is available from the
British Library

ISBN 978 1 902471 16 7

Book concept by Lady Mary Peters

Text by the sportswomen themselves, edited by
Derek Gallop

Design by Mike Brain at Wild Boar Design

Publishing and project management by
Chris Andrews

Printed by Pureprint Group Ltd.

Distribution by Gateway Publishing Ltd and
Chris Andrews Publications Ltd
15 Curtis Yard, North Hinksey Lane
Oxford OX2 0LX

Tel +44 (0)1865 723404
www.cap-ox.com
Info@gatewaysark.co.uk

All information including statistics in this book were correct at time of interviewing and printing